SOULMATE SETBACKS

Confessions II

Cover design: J. René Creative

Silhouette: © Untashable / Shutterstock

Editor: Burden of Proofreading

To my "*sane single women* who struggle to deal with *insane single men*..." you're not alone. We're all in this pissy ass dating pool together!

CHAPTER 1
the morning after

So after two, long, arduous years of celibacy by choice, I lie here questioning my decision-making abilities. This man brought me s'mores and vitamin water. That, by no means, should warrant visitation to my special lady palace. Many men who have had more to offer than chocolatey sweet treats haven't even made it past the palace gates, but Diego just *does* something to me that causes me to behave in a manner contrary to my sensible nature.

DING DING

I reach over in a slight haze to find my phone, thinking maybe it's Diego texting me something naughty about our recent activities. But alas, it's just Ariah.

Ariah: So you'd call to wake me when your dysfunctional ass neighbors used to have sex but not when YOU finally are!? Really bitch?

OMG, here we go.

Ariah: So how many times did he beat them knees!? Cuz you needed it!

Renée: Just once

Ariah: Oh okayyy, like once at the top of every hour or…?

Renée: Like ONCE once

Ariah: As in ONE TIME!?

Renée: I hate you.

Of course my phone is now ringing because she wants all the scoop. Who cares that it's officially booty call hours? And she must really want to know because, *if it can be texted, then why are you calling?* is her entire lifestyle.

I answer, "Yo."

"So what happened? I thought you was gon' tell me he waxed that ass like The Karate Kid!"

"You're an ass." I chuckle. "I got nothin', girl. We did it, it was fine… It was. Then that was it," I state blankly.

"Are you intentionally being ambiguous and obtuse?"

"Bitch, if you don't take your $90 grad school words somewhere *else* at 3 a.m.," I laugh. "And no. It was all goin' fine. He moves like a stripper, so that was fun. But once it went… away, it never fully came… *back*. Ya know? I guess he needed a *much* longer recovery time."

"Ohhhhh… Oh." Ariah is so rarely silent, but there is a long pause. "Soooo did youuu… ya know… to help it back up?"

"Let's just say I did all I was gonna do in that situation because I shouldn'ta been sleeping with him in the *first* place. Like damn, he bought me some s'mores," I laugh. "That doesn't earn back my years of lost trust."

"I mean you ain't wrong, but he does *you*."

And she ain't wrong either. He does me *very* well. However, I used to return that favor with gusto and had him just as sprung out – on my floor twitchin' and stutterin' and shit. Don't get it twisted, this strong trumpet playin' mouth can handle business. Hell, I've even given some friends a few tips of the trade – paying it forward since my Godmother taught me. For years, I thought that's what *every*one's Godmother did; like that was perfectly normal. *Siiigh, it's not.* But using a giant popsicle, she gave me some very useful tips. She also said to cover a banana in peanut butter, then remove said condiment without leaving teeth marks in the banana. She also taught me a method to continue "service" through his orgasm that makes it appear as though his flowing essence is being swallowed, but it's not. That way, everyone is happy.

Those skills were being put to use fairly regularly before Diego's first surprise engagement and him ghosting me. So there I was, dumb as hell, being intimate with *only* him and he's courting at *least* one other chick putting his dick who knows where – and then in *my* mouth? You got the wrong one, sir. I'm done. And his thick, smooth piece has not been blessed by these pouty lips since. You want it back? Earn back the trust; put in some damn work for a change.

One guy who was trying to smash but not actually *date* me said I have my stuff all locked up like Rapunzel. *Damn right!* That prince put in mad overtime for that chick. He fought a whole battle for her hairy ass! The prince can do all that while professing his love and I can't even get dinner? That doesn't work for me.

"Ok, well that was deep. Valid, but deep," Ariah agrees.

"Plus, this is so dumb, but my fertility specialist requires testing every six months. Like, they literally won't provide services without updated paperwork. So there is nowhere on my sexy chocolate body that this man will put his mouth and have to worry about leaving with an STD that will eat through his nasal cavity. Bitch, the Quest Diagnostics blood draw lab emblazoned a "**GRADE A**" stamp on my ass last month!"

Ariah laughs, "You are *so* dumb!"

"So who told you about this anyway?" I ask.

"Jenna."

"Didn't even know y'all had each other's phone numbers, but I didn't *tell* her. So who did?"

"Yeah, we exchanged at the infamous massage party that never happened. I think she said Brie told her."

Like seriously? My special sugar lump has inspired a whole damn phone tree!? Wonderful.

"So, why do you sound like that?" I ask. "You sound funny – congested or weird or something."

After a long silence, Ariah reluctantly explains how her TMJ disorder is still acting up and how she got lock jaw a few days prior.

"Ooooh! Please tell me you just yawned real big and it locked up on you," I ask, hoping for the best.

"Girl you *know* I was over here givin' that fire fellatio! But a yawn would've made a way better explanation to the chiropractor... and the dentist," she says, laughing.

"You *told* them that!?"

"Look bitch, I possess zero shame in my head game. Thank you and good night."

And with that, the line goes dead while I make a mental note to stretch and do some jaw massage prior to any future oral activities, since I'm so out of practice.

I drive into work full of anger, hatred, and fury. Regardless of the fact that I enjoy new cars and lease the most updated, fully loaded vehicle on the Moon Township Hyundai lot, I absolutely abhor driving. There's just something about everyone being in my way that incites all of my road rage, and I am thoroughly convinced I am one of the many reasons gun laws exist. If you're going slower than me in a passing lane, I should legally be allowed to shoot out one of your rear tires. But since that's not a thing, I continue to tailgate the slow ass driver in front of me until she gets the good sense to move over.

Work is really the absolute last place I care to be, considering I hold a position that doesn't actually require me to be in an office to do it. I'm on the creative end of a marketing team, so as long as I have the Adobe Creative Suite and a good Wi-Fi connection, I'm gravy, baby! My entire team can actually work remotely, however the higher-ups are old school and don't care to give us that option, so into the flames of torturous despair I go.

Today should be ok though. Since we're expecting a new staff member to join the team, we'll have a fun lunch out of the office. Not sure how well he's going to function once he meets our crazy crew. We are a highly inappropriate group of people – but in an amusing unstable way. During the last meeting, James, the manager of an equally dysfunctional department, had a whole discussion with me during a meeting with our team about my colleague Dani's *bush*! We were literally talking about the green leafy structure outside of Dani's house that was ruined by the landscaper, but when a random colleague walks past the office and hears James comment on how Dani's *bush* is no longer thick, it makes one think we should hold all of our meetings in the Human Resources office.

I have finally made it past the one-lane stretch of my commute to work, so I can now pass the slower drivers. The car in front of me and I are both doing 72 mph up a hill with a 40 mph speed limit, but it's ok because my middle name is Mario Andretti and I *live* for this speed!

"FUUUCK!!! FUCK!"

I have no idea what it was, but I just hit it! Well, that's a lie. The driver in front of me hit it and since I was tailing him only one car length behind, I immediately ran *over* it – so hard that I could hear my car hit the ground. I am immediately saddened because whatever it was didn't deserve to die in that horrifically unexpected manner. But my thoughts then shift to, *shit, what type of damage was done to my baby's undercarriage by that large animal?* I fear this is not going to be cheap.

Once I park, I walk around the car to survey the destruction. The tire and rim both appear to be unscathed, and the front end is fine, but the entire driver's side of my magnificent silver beauty looks like a crime scene. There is blood spanning just above the tire, across the whole left side, as far back as the trunk. My co-workers who've yet to arrive are going to think I murdered someone, but there is nothing I can do about it now. I'll just have to stop at the indoor carwash on the way home.

Upon entering my office, I find that Dani is early for a change and chatting with the new guy, Everett. My first thought is, I should probably buy extra cases of bottled water and canned goods because the world is coming to an end – this woman is *never* on time! We make our introductions and I welcome him to the team, while silently wishing him luck on his survival.

Everett is a visual enigma. Looking at him, one would assume that he's a super conservative guy with his button-down shirt buttoned all the way *up* and crisp khaki pants. His pale complexion, thick-framed glasses and clean cut appearance strongly resemble Clark Kent. Honestly, I was kind of waiting for him to rip open his shirt to reveal a giant red "S" on his chest, but I hold my tongue, for once, and don't vocalize that.

When he finally slides his chair from his desk, we notice he's rockin' crisp, new, limited-edition, custom Nike's with his nickname, E. Money, stitched on the sides. And once he really gets talking, he's nowhere near conventional, so hope is strong that he'll fit right in with us weirdos.

He shows us photos of his wife and asks, "So I know Dani's married. But what about you, Renée?"

"Hahhaaaaaaa haa hahaaaa," Dani howls. "But I did hear Diego was over last night..."

"I'm standing right *here*, you trash bucket! That's enough laughter at my expense. And who *told* you that!?"

"I woke up to a text from Brie," she admits, shrugging her shoulders.

Siiigh... I direct my attention to Everett, "No. Despite what Miss ABC News says over there, I'm single as a Pringle, boo. Got any sexy, solo, chocolate friends for me?"

Before he can reply, Dani jumps in. "She has the *worst* dating life, but her stories bring so much joy to everyone around her."

Chuckling in shock, he replies, "That's so terrible! I'm sorry, I don't have any chocolate friends. I didn't grow up in the most *diverse* area."

"So how *was* your weekend, Renée?" Dani deviously interjects with a smirk, alluding to my time with Diego, I'm sure. But I'm not about to traumatize the new guy with my tales from the dark side – not yet, anyway.

My weekend. It was *so weird*! I tell them about a friend request I received on social media from a handsome Black gentleman.

"Well, that's promising," Everett interjects.

Dani shakes her head. "And *I* promise, it's probably *nowhere* near promising." She grabs a five-dollar bill out of her purse and slaps it onto his desk. "I got five on it. Continue."

Everett waits a beat to see if she's serious, then removes a five from his own wallet to match hers. If this is part of the new office culture, he doesn't want to be excluded. Meanwhile, I'm just watching as these assholes bet cash money on how "promising" this prospect is.

I confess, I spied a bit before deciding if I would accept the stranger's request because I'm really particular about who I allow into my social space. My investigation confirmed that this is the same guy my sister, Neka, once told me about, suggesting I should date him. She then proceeded to tell me *she* had slept with him years ago, but it was cool because… nope, the reason doesn't even matter. Not really that cool.

He was well-built and clean-cut, but looked a lot younger than me. Also, he had some facial jewelry and always wore one dangling earring. Overall, based on the public content on his page, he wasn't really my type, even if he hadn't slept with my sister ages ago.

When I called her to inquire why this man was friending me, she told me that she was supposed to convince me to have a threesome.

"With *who*!?"

Hard pause. "Me and him," she laughed.

I wish we would've been on a video call so she could see my face all balled up. I'm not giving it to any *one* person, let alone another who I'm actually *related* to.

"Gross! Ew. I'm so confused! Plus, you're not even my type! So if I *had* to bed a chick, you ain't it."

"Fuck you *mean* I ain't your *type*!?" she asks incredulously. This girl was extra insulted that I would prefer to sleep with a woman *other than her* because in her mind, ain't no sexier bitch alive!

"OMG that is *not* the part you should be focused on right now! You're my *sister*! Incest is *not* best – for me anyway."

"Well I already told him you wasn't gon' be down for it, but he still thinks he can get you. I told him you was picky as hell and I wished him luck."

Everett blinks three times with raised eyebrows as if to say, *WTF did I just hear*, and nonchalantly hands Dani the ten dollars in defeat.

"Yeah, so that's my cue to get coffee. Where can I find coffee? Something strong and black."

"How Renée likes her men," Dani quips. "Right this way. I'll show you."

Before leaving, Everett turns back and asks, "Did you accept the request?"

"I did. Kinda curious to see how it plays out."

As they head over to the kitchen, the new guy is undoubtedly thinking I'm the strangest person he's ever met.

♀ ♂ ♀ ♂

We let Everett pick the place to dine for lunch.

"I'll drive if anyone wants to ride with me," I offer, completely forgetting about the early morning vehicular manslaughter event.

My manager, Kathy, promptly declines because she was thoroughly convinced she was going to meet her maker the last time she rode with me. But new guy and Dani don't know any better yet, so they allow me to chauffeur. Using my app, I remote start my car to warm it up and heat the seats so it'll be comfy upon our arrival.

As we approach the car, the gruesome blood spatter brings the earlier incident to my memory when they both stop dead and look, first at each other, then at me.

"Umm, should we have hitched a ride with Kathy? Because thissss issss... uh..." Everett says.

"Yeah, I completely forgot I ran over a deer this morning. I'm taking her to the car wash after work. It's ok, hop in."

Slowly they get in, both on the passenger side since the driver's side handles, particularly the back, are covered in blood.

We take off on our fifteen-minute drive to the restaurant. As we're talking and laughing, the car continues to heat up, blowing warm air on high throughout the interior. We begin to notice an abnormal smell that prompts Dani to look around to assess if someone tooted in the hot car. I notice it too and begin to recall every step of my morning routine – I know I put deodorant on today, that can't be me.

A few minutes later, it's clear that Everett notices as well when he breaks the awkward silence to ask, "Is there a reason your car *literally* smells like the *death* of the hopes and dreams of a thousand underprivileged children?"

Well, damn. We can't help but to laugh at the way he worded all that when he could've just said, "Hey why's your car stink?"

I pull off into the next available shopping complex and we all exit to inspect the car. Totally grossed out, we find a giant piece of unidentified beast carcass hanging from the underside, riding along with us while the heating system is pulling its stench inside. Blood covered bone and wet matted fur are not what anyone wants to see before lunch.

I drop them off at the restaurant and skip lunch to take my car to a local mechanic where not one but two men remove multiple chunks of animal. I told them I ran over a deer, but once they remove a foot-long chunk, they inform me that the fur is way too long and I did not hit a deer, but maybe a wolf or a coyote.

After I leave the mechanic, I go through the carwash and select the undercarriage power wash, yet my beautiful car still reeks like the death of a thousand suns!

Add to my TO-DO list: Find a job in the city where I won't run over the damn animal kingdom

CHAPTER 2
medical mishaps

I have found a new therapist. While the last one was nice, she wasn't effective or helpful. Starting our sessions with, "tell me what's going on," would be fine if we were actually accomplishing something and I was leaving with solid techniques to stabilize my work-related stress and anxiety. Plus, she would make faces if anything was said that she didn't agree with. *Hi, um pardon me, ma'am, but I'mma need for you to get your face together while you realize that my life's decisions are not being presented for your approval.* Moving on.

Remember Thomas? The guy who overindulged in the bourbon at the cigar bar? Well, he referred me to his Black *male* therapist. Never had one of those before, so maybe it's time to try something new. My work stress has been at an all-time high, but thankfully not high enough to chop all of my hair off again. I barely touch scissors to even cut *paper* after that incident.

I Googled him prior to calling and setting my first appointment and holy shit. That man is *fine!*

There is no way I can tell this person my innermost thoughts and disruptive feelings. He's going to think I'm a total sociopath if I tell him that I work daily to resist the urge to kick certain people down a flight of the closest stairs – while they're on fire. So I knew in that moment I needed to find someone else. My dietician searched. My office health coach searched. I searched. But our overly extensive quest for a Black female therapist was not working in anyone's favor. Many we found were Christian based, and we all know I curse too much to be sharing my unsavory stories and questionable issues with a woman of God. So I broke down and called this gorgeous man to attempt to therapize me into normalcy. All I can do is wish him luck on those days my depression decides to creep in to inform me that, *bitch you ain't shit, nobody decent will ever want you, and you will definitely die alone.* Somebody for real needs to choke that voice.

So far, his techniques seem solid and he definitely leaves me with things to reflect upon and think about, but my thoughts almost always end up deviating to the wayward dark place.

This beautiful dark chocolate man is saying words to me. Is it wrong that I want to lick my computer screen right now? His broad muscular shoulders span the width of my eighteen-inch laptop monitor for this video appointment. His biceps look like they are fighting each other to escape from his well-fitted sleeves. *Oh man, if my nipples get hard, I can always cut my video feed and feign technical difficulties. Phew... Cuz I am DEFinitely having some difficulties. Concentrate!*

I am in a trance-like state watching his perfectly full, well-moisturized lips move. Then he smiles at the end of a sentence, which makes me melt into a puddle of sexual chocolate. Whyyy oh whyyy does that beautiful smile compliment his supple lips so well? It's just not natural. *Shit, these words he's saying – I should be paying better attention to them. They're probably important and beneficial to my overall well-being. I wonder if his deep, almond-shaped eyes can see that I'm diligently fighting to not show blatant lust all over my very expressive face? Focus Renée!*

Most people who interact with me think I'm kind of quirky, but otherwise well-adjusted. They often ask, *why do you need therapy? You're not crazy?* Well, newsflash, you don't have to be crazy to get therapy. But reason #284.6 article C of why I *should* probably be under *some*one's mental health care is because of my psychotic ass parents.

As a child, I would overhear my mother and her best friend of over fifty years, who happens to be my Godmother, talking about a little man in the tunnel. Yes, *that* tunnel, as in my special lady tunnel. Apparently inside of my miniature yum yum box – before she became a full grown snack box, there is a little man who resides and has an entire furnished apartment. According to these grown women, when a lady becomes physically aroused, the little man in the tunnel moves all of his furniture out of the way to accommodate the "guest" who will be running in and out of the house, so to speak. And then once it's all over and the guest leaves for good, the little man in the tunnel puts his furniture back and continues to live his best life. As an impressionable youth, overhearing two grown ass women have this discussion, for *years* I was afraid to jump because I thought a little person was gonna come falling out.

So now when my therapist asks what I'm looking for in a relationship? Absolutely a portion of my answer is going to be sexual attraction strong enough that the little man in my tunnel is throwing lamp shades and coffee tables out of my golden box in anticipation for my guest of honor. I want an entire couch, cushions and all, to come tumbling out of there. But I can't say that in therapy because this man will have me locked up somewhere in a padded cell.

I don't feel like I was eavesdropping, but my Godmother, rest her soul, was a very boisterous and vocally robust woman whose voice carried. So when they were having conversations about Herman and Eloise, I was privy to all of that inappropriateness.

Oh, who is this fine couple you ask? Genital herpes – they named them Herman and Eloise. Apparently, when *they* were in college, there was a girl at the bar who was "fast." I didn't know any better – I thought that simply meant she was a decent track and field athlete. They joked that when she would take a bath, Herman and Eloise didn't want to drown, so they hopped up onto the side of the bathtub to wait until the bath was complete. *What?* I maintain that these are two solid reasons why, throughout college, I remained celibate and didn't engage in casual sex because I didn't want an ottoman and bookshelf falling out of my lady condo and have Herman and Eloise watching me bathe. My childhood was an entire abomination. Lots of love, but a hot mess, nonetheless.

"I'm sorry, can you repeat that please?" I ask. *EXACTLY! Because you weren't paying attention, Renée – too busy enjoying his strong jaw-line!*

Before answering, I give my smokin' counselor's question some thought, but I'm also pondering how I'd love nothing more than to rub on his head and make a wish for three more who look just like him! He wears a ring, but is he really married or is it just so his female patients don't hit on him? I don't think he's gay, but anything is possible.

"I'm lonely because I'm waiting for that Heathcliff and Clair Huxtable laughable love. That

Gomez and Morticia Addams heat, intensity and passion. Barack and Michelle's support, respect and adoration for one another. And the little man in the tunnel to go nuts! I really don't feel like I should have to settle for that much less. I feel like those are normal attributes for people in love and devoted to one another."

He nods. "You're not wrong, but you might have to leave town to find it," he laughs. "Wait, what's this about a little man?"

♀ ♂ ♀ ♂

I close my computer and run upstairs to freshen up. I took a "mental health day" from work to get in some of these appointments that I've been intentionally delaying. Even though I drink more water than is humanly necessary, my kidneys are acting funky and I'm about seven months past due for my well woman visit, so I'm convinced that it's all just falling apart down there. So one appointment down, two to go, and then I'll meet Frank – another online suitor with whom I've been chatting for a few days.

The last visit *any* woman wants to make is to the annual "lady Doc." But it's a necessary evil and Dr. Morgan, though rarely on time because of her thoroughness, at least makes it bearable. So while I wait on the exam table, I continue reading my new Norian Love novel that had recently arrived. I must admit, I'm finding myself becoming increasingly physically aroused and if my womanhood maintains this level of excitement, the Doc's bound to notice something happening down there. So I abruptly close the book and shove it back into my purse for later reading.

The slender, petite brunette enters the room for my pre-exam discussion and informs me that my blood pressure is elevated. I inquire what to do about it, like *she's* the right person to ask.

"Your PCP will likely suggest some lifestyle changes."

"Well, short of changing my entire sexual orientation, there's not much about my actual lifestyle I can alter – I eat and drink healthy, workout every day..."

She looks at my paperwork I had just filled out with a raised eyebrow and says, "Well... uuuhhh... It looks like it's *been* a while so *mayyy*beeee..."

Clearly I forgot to mention my most recent "activity" a few weeks back. But did my doctor really just recommend *sex* to lower my blood pressure? Because if so, I'm all the way down with that! Now, if she could prescribe me a functional man without commitment issues, that would be tremendously helpful.

The one I'd spoken to the other night told me he's an investor – but doesn't drive. Man, if you don't take your ass on and invest in a *vehicle*!? Living deep in the suburbs where there is no public transportation, informing me that, "We can meet for a drink; you can pick me up." You, sir, are on all of the drugs! Last I checked, I still don't drive for Uber. Grown ass men drive grown ass cars. Period. Doesn't even have to be new, just be able to meet me somewhere. Being chivalrous enough to pick me up would be even better, but if I hold my breath waiting for *that* shit, I'll pass out.

So after she calls her assistant in, Dr. Morgan has me assume the position to prepare for this invasion, I mean, exam. She angles that giant construction-like flood-light in my direction to thoroughly illuminate my lady essence. I lie there, ready to be medically violated, but there is only silence. I notice her head rise from between my legs to look over the sheet that's draped across my knees, glance over to her assistant who smirks, then back at me.

"Renée, um, is this... *glitter*?"

"Well yeah! I wanted her to look great for you, Doc." The new Victoria's Secret glitter lotion is designed to make *everything* shimmer and pop.

"Yeah, uh, ok. So... thank you for your cleanliness and beautification rituals, however sparkles aren't necessary in this particular situation... And are you referring to your vagina in the third person?"

"Absolutely. She's a rare blossoming specimen to behold. Does she look good? Is she looking healthy? Is everything in the right place?" *It should be since she's not used often.*

The good doctor refocuses her attention to begin the exam. "Your entire... outside region looks... yes. Visually, all good." The assistant is passing her the necessary instruments while trying her best to maintain her professionalism and not outwardly laugh at our exchange. I have to be, by far, the most memorable patient any of my doctors have ever seen.

"So. I know you prefer a call with test results, so you'll hear from us as soon as they're in."

Normally this is when she thanks me and leaves, but she instead remains seated. "What's going on with the whole baby situation? You're at an age where... ya know..."

Ugh... Thanks for the reminder. "Yeah, I've been seeing Dr. Scott and we're exploring options for conceiving myself since every man I seem to meet is all wrong. Dr. Morgan, a man tried to holla at me the other day – he was using not one but *two* canes. If he *did* get it up, who's gonna hold *him* up to give it to me?"

She laughs and wishes me the best of luck. At this rate, I'm gonna need it. Just a few nights ago, I ended up getting hung up on by a guy who said that hypothetically if our child were gay, he would disown him and put him out because he should know better. Really!? Then hypothetically, *we* will *never* reproduce together because what you're *not* about to do is throw *my* child out into the street because of your close-mindedness. I love how he then had the nerve to be offended by my overly maternal statement before he hung up on me. Everyone's entitled to their own views on things, but unconditional love for my future child is not a viewpoint that is up for debate.

♀ ♂ ♀ ♂

Two down, one to go. Because Dr. Morgan was so late, I'm cutting it close arriving to my last appointment on time. And of course, parking would be trash during the early afternoon. But I make it to the urologist just in time.

This is my first time visiting this type of specialist; so basically, I'm getting old. There is no one under seventy-five in the waiting room with me, which makes me feel even older.

The technician takes me in for an x-ray, and in my natural germophobic manner, I'm looking around and seeing all kinds of craziness in this room that would make it *far* from a sterile environment. Not that you necessarily need a sterile atmosphere for a scan, but it would be nice since we're in a hospital and all.

There is that baby blue, textured, plastic suitcase that *everyone's* grandma owned that was heavily in style in the forties, outdated wallpaper that is beginning to peel, all the equipment looks due for an upgrade, and the remaining space is cluttered with stacked boxes. To top it off, a crusty-looking IV bag is just chillin' beside me with goodness only knows what or whose fluid inside!

I am then asked to pee in some free-standing structure that is housed in the same room as the ultrasound – not a toilet, though. It simply has four curtains around it for "privacy." To wipe, this ultrasound tech hands me *Kleenex*! Did they forget to tell this chick that toilet paper exists for a reason? Also, there isn't even a trash can beside me. Where is it? Across the damn room! So she comes in to read the results and dispose of the urine. Where does she pour it? Naturally, in the sink! Yes, that would be the same sink where we both recently washed our hands! How do I know the previous person's creepy urine didn't splash up on the handle that I just touched? I want to wipe my *whole* body down with a Clorox wipe after this hot mess.

Once that fresh hell is over, they recommend some strange surgical procedure to explore. I ask the lady, "Where would the doctor do the procedure?"

"Oh, right here in this room," she says, like any of that makes sense. *Aww helll naw*! Time to go. Care to guess what I *don't* need? Yeah, hepatitis. I smile at that woman, promptly gather my belongings, and get out of there as quickly as possible without scheduling that procedure. I will sooner let my entire kidney fall out and get eaten by a pack of wild dingoes before allowing them to insert anything into my body that came from that creepy, contaminated office.

♀ ♂ ♀ ♂

I get all dressed up in something casual-cute to meet Frank. Thank heavens I'm still strongly attached to these ice cream dates because I would never make it through a meal with this man.

Ever watch the show Criminal Minds? It's the scripted drama that's heavily focused on the most sadistic serial killers one could ever imagine. Frank could've starred in the episode where the guy was removing the skin off of women's toes for fun. I don't even know if that was a storyline, but the way Frank looks, it probably could've been one! His bulging blue eyes that always seem intently focused on something random... The unruly nature of his furrowed brows... The one tuft of hair that runs down the center of his chin... The Hannibal Lecter-ish grin hiding yellow teeth... The black turtle neck covering his lanky body on a seventy-degree evening... This was not the vibe I got from his photos so nope, I'm good. I suck down that ice cream so fast that I give myself a headache, making the perfect excuse to escape early, all limbs still intact. And to ensure they *stay* that way, I take the most roundabout way home possible to guarantee I'm not being followed.

Add to my TO-DO list: Upgrade my security system ASAP

CHAPTER 3
i think i'm straight

"Harder... OMG right therrrre!"

"Here?"

"Yassss, oh shit... deeper! Ugh! That's the spot! Gahhh, you're sooo good at this," I moan.

"Bitch, I've been massaging you weekly for *twelve years*! I know what you like," my massage therapist Blaire boasts arrogantly. "But the fact that you make it sound more like porn than a therapeutic back massage is why we have to do this in the basement! What would your neighbors think if they heard your cries of ecstasy? Oh wait. I forgot who I was talking to."

I hate her so much!

"It's so *warm* in here right now," she comments. "How is your body so *cold*?"

"It's the demon living inside me. He's cold."

"Oh... ok," she nods and doesn't miss a massage beat, like everything I just said was perfectly normal. I *think* she knows I'm joking.

"Leave me alone and let me enjoy my self-care, please. This feels better than sex anyway," I whimper in a woozy state.

"Then *you*, my dear, are having the wrong kind of sex!"

Ooooh child, she ain't lyin'! But at this rate, I'm never gettin' any again in my life. I regale Blaire with the story of a recent first date with Pierre. Not my usual type, but clearly I haven't learned my lesson, so I'm still out here giving people chances who probably shouldn't have them.

My curly thick hair had been straightened and was sleekly flowing down to the middle of my back. Contacts in, face beat, and ready for business. I had meticulously selected the navy blue, empire-waist maxi dress with a deep gold Mayan-esque stitching across my very large bust, with a similar subtle stitching continuing down the length of the dress. It flowed well, but hugged my upper body in all the right places. My cleavage was going to announce my presence well before I could even arrive with the infamous glitter body cream simultaneously scenting them and making them sparkle. Matching gold sandals and the Mayan stone necklace that my bestie Liza bought me from her travels accented my look. *You smell good. You look good. Let's do this!*

I grabbed my keys to throw in my wristlet and stepped outside to greet this new man. His bright smile faded as he looked me up and down and said, "I don't like that dress. Go change."

Shit, there goes my whole face again.

"WHOOOOO THE FUUUUCK DOES HE THINK HE ISS?!" Blaire yells as she slams her hands down on the massage table, barely missing my leg and momentarily stopping my heart. "With a name like Pierre, I would expect a little more class!"

"*Right*!? I told him I will most certainly *not* go change. I looked good in that dress!" I yell in agreement. "He had on dress shoes with no socks and telling *me* to go change! We're going mini golfing. *You* go change! Then he had the audacity to tell me to never wear that dress again."

I mean, it may not be *everyone's* favorite item of clothing to look at, but I lost forty-one pounds! By *no* means did I look jacked up enough in this dress to the point where I should be told to never wear it again. My waist was snatched and my skin was bronzed. He could kiss the blackest part of my ass.

Pierre was going to drive that day, and the outfit I *initially* had laid out to wear was *all* white. However, the interior of his white-on-white Dodge Challenger was visibly filthy, so there was no way in hell I was ruining my crisp white shit in his dirty ass car! So I would've had to change into what I was wearing anyway.

We awkwardly played our mini golf while his bare feet sweat through his shoes, no doubt. Oddly enough, I received four compliments on my dress from random women, which made me feel sexier than *he* did all night, with not one single admiring comment paid to me the entire date.

I reluctantly agreed to accompany him to grab coffee and dessert after, but when he was going to only tip 10% when we had *really* solid service, despite him speaking to our server recklessly? Nope. I can't even deal with someone who is unnecessarily disrespectful to people. Besides, we were at Eat 'N Park – 20% would've only been $3.80. Dude, get your *life* together and, at the very least, tip right! Thank heavens I had cash on me and was able to slip her a five on top of the change he left.

"OMG, so he's insulting, sweaty, *and* cheap?! I don't care who you are, that leaves a terrible impression! You don't tip badly on a first date!"

"You don't tip badly *ever*," I state in solid agreement.

"True. Well I have seen you in that dress before, and you looked beautiful in it. I just wanna punch his throat out."

"Right!? Thank you! I definitely don't think it's the worst or homeliest thing I own."

"Knowing you, I doubt you own anything homely... except these big ass granny panties you got on! What is *happening* here? Go Change!" she commands in laughter, imitating Pierre.

Still unsure why, but he stayed on my porch talking to me until one in the morning. So he wasn't *not* interested, just not enough to say anything nice to me. I am so over these fucking men!

Blaire continues to massage me, taking out her frustration on my poor skinny calves – assuring me if I keep hope alive, that one day I'll find my match. *I wonder what she's been smoking?*

♀ ♂ ♀ ♂

At the end of every massage, it is customary for me to throw a tantrum because, while Blaire may be finished massaging me for the time I've paid for, *I'm* not done! Ninety minutes goes by way too quickly and I maintain that if and when I fall asleep during said massage, those minutes shouldn't count and she should have to start over. Regardless of how often I plead my case, she's not hearing it and treats me like a whole toddler. She walks away chuckling while I throw my fit.

As we ascend the basement stairs and make our way out to the porch, Blaire takes a seat. "Care if I hang for a few on your awesome porch, mamas?"

That's odd, she never stays to chill after a massage – what a treat! I grab her a bottle of water and we chat as the cars roll past – and through the stop sign as usual.

"So this guy yesterday said he would massage me, but he doesn't do feet," I casually mention to Blaire. "I have nice feet, buddy! There's no hammer time here."

"Dude seriously doesn't know what he's missing! You should have told him that podiatrists pay *you* to come in to touch your Greek goddess feet!"

"Exactly!"

"So. How's therapy going?" she inquires. "I heard your new counselor is a whole snack!"

"Who *told* you that?"

"Jenna had a massage a few days ago. I *also* heard you had to buy a new computer because he burned right through it," she says with an eyebrow raise.

I sit, staring blankly, shaking my head on the inside. Everyone's got jokes. It seems like these women are the ones who need therapy more than I do.

I don't recognize the number when the phone rings, but stupid here answers it anyway – always on speakerphone, fully intending to ask the caller if I can get back with them once my company leaves.

"Ooh, is it a man?" she asks, peeking over toward the phone.

Beats me. "Hello?"

"Heyyy girrl…" The caller has a deeper voice, but not one that I immediately recognize. I can tell it's not a man, though.

I hesitate. "Hi… to whom am I speaking?"

"Oh my fuck, you're so damn proper," Blaire whispers, laughing. I flip her off.

"This Rachael," she says in a clearly urban tone.

I shrug my shoulders at Blaire because I have no clue who this is. I don't know a Rachael.

She continues, "Kiara said you was expectin' my call."

Still super confused because Kiara is my hair stylist. She pressed out my hair the other day for an event, but she didn't say anything about having anyone call me.

"Oh, so she referred you to me for graphic design work for your business," I reply confidently. Because why else would a random woman be calling me? Right? Wrong… Again.

"I don't got a bizness, but I'm tryin' to get in *your* bizness though."

"Wait, what? Excuse me? Who are you?"

Blaire's eyes are as big as saucers as Rachael continues, "Kiara said we'd make a nice couple and to give you a call. So I think we should link up, ya know?"

"Nooo, sorry, I *don't* know. I'm not sure why Kiara gave you my number, but I'm straight."

Rachael laughs. "Sure you are."

I'm making facial expressions at the phone like she can see me. As politely as I can, I inform her, "My hair was done for an upcoming event – with a man – a man I'm sleeping with. I'm sorry you were misinformed, but thanks for your call. Goodbye." I hang up.

Not *really* sleeping with him, but she doesn't need to know that. The point is, I don't currently swing that direction. But the way these men are behaving, I feel like my lesbian friends may have the right idea.

"OHH EMMM GEE!" Blaire is blown away. "Did I just hear that correctly? Your hair stylist gave your phone number to a woman and basically alluded to the fact that you were a lesbian!? Who *does* that!?"

And she *knows* I'm straight as an arrow encased in concrete! Like, am I being Punk'd here!? A good while back when she did my hair, I *told* her I was flying out to see my ex, Marshall, in California – just for a visit, nothing romantic. She didn't know all the specifics, but the point is, Marshall has a large, thick, beautiful, mocha *penis*! And he was so good with *all* of his appendages that he had me hiding out in his bathroom calling Dr. Morgan at 6am, their time. I awkwardly voiced my concerns about why during oral sex, I had to fight him off of me because I had an overwhelming feeling that I needed to pee. It made no sense considering I always empty my bladder, then shower before allowing anyone to taste my forbidden fruit.

This poor doctor was explaining to a naïve grown ass woman – me – about female ejaculation, a.k.a. squirting, how it's not urine, and that I should feel grateful to have a man skilled enough to cause such an extreme physical reaction. *Well damn. Even Diego couldn't do that.*

But I didn't care what she said, I was not gonna let loose and accidentally pee or whatever on this man's face! I really *liked* him!

No sooner do I finish telling Blaire that story, the phone rings again – same number. She doesn't even wait for me to say "hello" before speaking.

"I fa real think you should reconsider. She showed me your pics and everything. You a li'l sexy and I think we could make sum'n work."

"Yeah, thank you again, but no thank you."

I hang up, immediately call Kiara, and demand to know what the actual fuck she was thinking, handing my number out and passing me off as the lesbian she *knows* I'm not. Hell, I would be just as pissed if she had handed my number out to a random man. Not cool.

Now, I *will* say I came to a few very startling sexual revelations watching Magic Mike XXL:

1. I *need* to have sex with a male exotic dancer at least *once* in my life because the things they can do with those hips are of an un*god*ly nature and I am *so* ok with that – we can pray about it later.

2. I questioned my sexuality for aboooooout twenty-three good seconds because I found Jada Pinkett-Smith just as hot as those men. Is that weird? Oh, who cares...

3. *If* she were to show up on my porch in that white pantsuit, I *might* have to let her in – just keepin' it real.

But Kiara didn't send me Jada. She sent Rachael, who Blaire found on Kiara's Facebook friends list. She's all wrong for me anyway!

Blaire listens in shock as this chick has the audacity to defend her actions and tell me she thought I liked girls and that Rachael and I would pair well together. The last time she did my hair *was* the last time she would ever do my hair. I immediately delete her contact information because that's just unprofessional.

The next morning, I wake up feeling refreshed after my massage. I throw on my favorite over-sized gray sweat suit and make my way downstairs for breakfast. Then I make the stupid decision to look at my phone and all the notifications bring on a fresh wave of tension. I can feel the tightness forming in my body that Blaire will have to fight with next week.

Not only has Rachael found me on Facebook, but has also begun to message me and send me what she probably perceives to be cute memes that reference how I don't know what I'm missing. She may very well be right, but I politely thank her again for her interest, while firmly letting her know that I do not currently return the sentiment, and I send her to the ignore list.

Also, why did the 45-year-old dude who lived with his mama and had no cable just find me on that damn dating site after two whole years!? This guy took me to his house, which I then immediately realized it wasn't *his* house because all the décor and furniture looked so old and matronly. There was still plastic on the cushions! When he asked if I wanted him to put in a video, as in a VHS tape that goes into a VCR, that was my cue. A *video!?!? Are you for real!? What year is it!?* There is an entire subset of people right now who don't even know what any of that means! If you don't take your ass online and get a Netflix subscription or, at the very least, head over to the Walmart and pick up one of those $19.88 DVD players...

My phone rings and a knot forms in the pit of my stomach as I realize I never blocked Rachael's number from my landline. To my relief, it's just Liza calling for one of our standard morning chats. I fill her in on the girly drama and know if I could only see her face, I'm certain she's doing that "in shock-blushing" thing she does.

"Also, why did I just get an online message from a man with three gold front teeth? I can't date you with three gold front teeth! Especially when you *look* like you would have three gold front teeth before you even open your mouth."

My best friend is literally about the sweetest person alive as she tries to justify his dental decisions. "Ohh, maybe it's one of those fake thingies that people put on the front."

She can't recall the word for grille, and I'm pretty sure it's not a gold grille, but adorable of her to try.

"Why is he texting you so early?"

"Online, not texting. You think I would really give my number to a man with a visible mass of golden teeth?"

All of this is so incredibly depressing. Liza has been happily married for like fifteen years; my other bestie Julia, for twenty. And Brie? She got married, had a child, divorced, dated, found a whole new man, got engaged, and he walked her happy ass on down the aisle *again*, all while I'm still trying to find just *one* decent man! Brie's hubby did some Hallmark movie shit taking her to an elegant dinner, then a helicopter ride where "MARRY ME" was spelled out in twinkling lights below in an open field. He then plopped a big ass beautiful ring on her finger. What!? He's out here making every man alive look bad, but sadly, they don't have to try too hard because I'm over here with the "Beat Your Meat Specialist" in my inbox, trying to reconnect with me. No, *I'm* not giving him that name. It was his actual account name that he chose all by his simple-ass-self. No one gets to call me picky ever again!

I fill Liza in on this man-child's particular meat specialty and the silence on the line clearly indicates her perpetual state of shock when talking to me. I read her his profile write-up:

Sheesh. My tagline is mainly tongue in cheek, but there is some truth behind it. In the last year, I've had to beat my meat so many times that I've developed new techniques. With that said, women I should not have become a specialist in the art of jacking off. You women make it so difficult for no reason. Look I know I'm not some Adonis or Fabio and I don't have an ego to the point to where I don't believe that no woman is out of my league but if I send you a message there is a 98%

chance that I don't think you are. Some of you women think you're God's gift to men and 95% of you aren't (I'll let you decide if you're in that 5%)

"Ok, so did he at least spell 'you're' correctly?" she asks with a hint of optimism, knowing full well he's not a match for her friend with actual standards.

"He did, oddly enough. But that's about it. Reading this, I just don't understand how he is able to control the hordes of women beating down his door to sauté his flappy meat sack. He sounds like a real catch."

"Oh yes," Liza says sarcastically. "So confident, yet sensitive and charismatic. I think we might have to hunt him down."

We won't have to. This dude messaged me and said he's been trying to date me for the past *ten years* and I wouldn't give him a chance. LIES! I talked to him *online* about eight months ago and he was very immature, so I wasn't interested.

He claimed that we'd spoken on the phone many times and that I showed him I could belch on command *very* long. LIES! Unless phone sex is involved, I would never intentionally make bodily noises on the phone with a man. I'm trying to *get* and *keep* a man, not run him off. Plus, even if I elected to, I *can't* do long purposeful belches so, there's that.

I supposedly said that we could meet at The Cheesecake Factory, but I stood him up. EXTRA LIES! Not only was there no Cheesecake Factory near me, but I prefer dessert to their actual meals, so I wouldn't have agreed to meet there for dinner. Not to mention that I have never stood a man up – ever. It's rude.

When I politely informed him he had the wrong woman, he called me a bitch and brought my biological clock into the conversation, which promptly got him blocked. This shit here is why he is the *Beat Your Meat Specialist*; no woman wants immature, childish, delusional "meat."

Add to my TO-DO list: Find a warm comfy hole to crawl into and die alone, because I can't keep this up for much longer

CHAPTER 4

i'm changing my name to "no"

My phone is literally ringing off the hook this morning. Most of the numbers are unfamiliar, so I'm thinking they're trying to get me to extend my car's warranty. You know, the one that I lease, so it's already covered bumper to bumper for the duration of my three-year term? But the one number looks so familiar, I decide to answer. What the hell was I thinking?

"Hello?"

"Morning baby, I got my test results. We can have sex now."

"Who the hell *is* this?"

I honestly feel like I know who it is, but I wasn't interested in him a year ago, definitely not interested now. What possesses a man to randomly call a woman he hasn't spoken to in ages, asking if he can just hop in the sack with her? I'm so confused. I think what confuses me even more is the fact that most men I meet *only* want me for sex. Never mind that I am highly educated, intelligent, super quirky, funny, down to earth and would make a great *actual* life partner. To them, I am basically just an available hole for their man missile. I could even see if the photos on my dating profile visibly indicated that I'm only here for some sexy time. But they don't. They are very tame compared to my actual personality, and my body is tastefully covered in all of them. I'm not giving the impression that I'm out here passing out my sweet treat to the male masses of Pittsburgh.

That would be the third time this level of craziness has happened recently. The other day, I had a gentleman ask me if we could have sex again if he brings over his STD paperwork. He then informed me he loves my body, the way I kiss, and ended with how amazing my snack box tastes, which caused me to almost vomit on the cat. I love having it done, but don't like to actually think about the details. I personally don't understand the appeal from the giver's end – particularly Diego's overwhelming need to do it. I would always ask him "why" in an effort to better understand, but the only response he'd ever give me is, "It's jus' different with you... *she's* different. And I love the way you come."

That immediately made me curious about *how* she's different and what separates *my* orgasms from other womens'. I did ask my friends a few random questions about their big O's, but it didn't provide much clarification. Hmmm, maybe *that's* why Kiara thought I was a lesbian. Either way, that particular desire still makes no sense to me.

Though I'm sure many would disagree, penises are right there, out in the open and way easier to deal with. Women are freaking weird. Female orgasms are like some enigma that should be studied by NASA. Our mental state should be in a "good place" – whatever the hell *that* means, lighting has to be right, temperature has to be between 68 and 71.52 degrees Fahrenheit, Mercury must be in retrograde, and we may require a full moon as the tide rolls in at dawn. Once all of these events have aligned, we can then achieve orgasm. I don't need those problems. Just hand me a penis, please. But I guess that's literally the problem. Everyone is trying to hand me their penis.

So Tony here thinks he can call me after an entire year and assumes that I will sleep with him because he finally got tested. The reality is sex with him was never even on the table – or anywhere else, for that matter. We went out once and his creepy teeth combined with his rancid breath and stale body scent, due to the excessive cigar smoking, put an end to any interest I might have entertained. He didn't want to get tested anyway, so the fact that he finally did leads me to believe he must've had a scare that forced him into it.

Unlike another gentleman I'd met who told me he gets tested regularly every quarter. Ummm, why? How much dick are you distributing in the tri-state area that you need to have your tool tested that often? That makes me feel more disconcerted than comforted, so sex with him was also off the table. In fact, the table said, "screw it," and found a new home.

While I was on the phone explaining to Tony why we would never be intimate, I missed a call from Desirée and a text message from Eli. He still randomly texts even though he's moved out of state.

Eli: When we gonna get started working on your list?

As the queen of multi-tasking, I reply to him while I return Desirée's phone call on my landline and make scrambled eggs.

Renée: What list?

"Hey girl, sorry I missed your call. Phone's been goin' crazy all morning and now this fool Eli is texting me. How are you?"

"Wait. He na the one who kept invitin' you to his house but na had furniture?" she asks in a way only she can with her thick island accent.

"But he had a whole deer head on his bedroom floor – no bed though? That's the one," I confirm.

Eli: Your bucket list. I wanna suck on your nips.

"Well what'at poor fool want?"

"Apparently to suck on my nips."

"Wait, what!? He *said* that? Did someone drop that chile on 'is head as a baby?"

"Girl, right!? I just replied that since I'm not really interested romantically, him, me, the bucket list, and the whole nip sucking aren't likely to happen."

Eli: What's wrong with me?

Isn't that the question of the damn year? But be nice.

Renée: Nothing is wrong with you. You're very handsome, especially with the new facial hair. But I just don't feel any spark or romantic connection when we're together. It's either there or it's not.

Eli: I still wanna suck on your nips

"Ok see, I'm dun wit'im! Tell'at man go buy a couch and si'down sumwhere!"

I laugh, "In one ear and out the other. He would've had better luck offering to spank me. We all know I'm more of a booty babe."

So basically, in the past *eight* minutes, two separate men have asked me for some form of sexual activity. Can guys really not tell when a woman is just not interested? Do we always have to come out and *verbally* say it? At this point, it's becoming increasingly difficult to maintain any level of tact because I'm *tired*.

As Desirée, in true fashion, offers services to put curses on these simple men, a loud bang on the door makes me jump and drop the house phone, with Des on the line, into the hot pan of almost cooked scrambled eggs. I fish it out and put her on speakerphone.

"Hold on girl, someone is banging on my back door."

"The back? Well I'm stayin' on the phone then. Cuz no one should be back there."

And she ain't lyin'. The way my home is set up, you have to walk up my driveway to get to the back door, so I never have people knocking back there. I peep through the blinds to meet the gaze of an unknown Black woman with a bag and a purse. It's a pretty chilly day, so she has on a black coat with what appears to be a green hoodie underneath with the hood up. The woman is also wearing a trash ton of makeup with dark brown leggings and yellow rain galoshes.

"I don't know who this is, but I'mma open the door to see what she wants. Stay on the phone." I then remind her of my address, just in case some shit pops off. Hell, Diego got bitches everywhere. This could be one of them.

As I open the door, I can now clearly see that this woman doesn't have any pants on! Those dark brown leggings? That's actually skin! She is wearing a hoodie, a pea coat and *no pants*!

"Hi I'm looking for a passtah," she says in what seems like an exasperated tone. "This the passtah's house? I need a passtah."

I'm assuming she thinks my house is the church parsonage since I live across the street from two separate churches in two different directions. But there are other homes much closer, so I'm not sure what made her select this one to hunt down a pastor.

"I'm sorry but this house doesn't belong to the church, but –"

"Well I been walkin' all over town lookin' for a passtah," she interrupts. "I can't just be out here walkin' this much cuz I got low iron! My iron is low!"

I can hear Des on the phone, saying, "wha' the?" and I'm thinking that exact same thing because as a people, we tend to overdress in cooler temps and this woman came out of her house or wherever *sans* pants! She has great legs though – so smooth I thought they *were* pants.

I give her what information I have regarding the two churches that are nearby and inquire why she specifically needs a pastor. Maybe I can direct her elsewhere for help because it's not even Sunday.

"I told you! I have low iron! I need a passtah!" And just like that, the pant-less lady stomps off across the street to my neighbor Ella's house, then finally to the church.

"Before you even ask, I have no idea what that was about," I direct my attention back to Des. "You have low iron levels; why does she need a pastor for that?"

"Chile, I take an iron pill for mine so I na got answers for you."

"You're lucky I didn't send her ass over to you. You could share your supplements with her," I joke, imagining how *that* interaction would go down.

The next few hours are spent watching the church, while I wait for a delivery, to make sure the female pastor comes out ok after a half-naked woman with low iron found her and entered the house of worship.

♀ ♂ ♀ ♂

After many delays and back orders, my bed is finally scheduled to arrive today! I remove and wash the current bedding and prep the room to receive my new special gift to myself. There really was nothing wrong with the previous mattress, but this one vibrates, has ambient lighting beneath, and bends and folds me in fun ways. Not that any of that matters because I'm still super single and will likely be celibate until my lady opening dries up and dies. But I still should put the restraint system back on, just in case. I imagine it's going to be a little awkward when I have to ask the delivery men to pause so I can make this last-minute addition. But it's okay, because we're all grown here. We know what it is. Right? *So. So. Wrong.*

A Hispanic child knocks on my door, no older than sixteen years of age. "We're here to deliver your mattress, ma'am," he says with an accent and an adolescent crack in his voice.

Shock is written all over my face. *Where are the grown men who handle this?* I peek out the door to figure out who drove this child to my house and see an older gentleman – his father. So a father/underage son duo is about to install a vibrating bed upon which I am going to place sex restraints. *Wonderful!*

Once they install the base, I put the bed skirt on and stall to see if the father will follow his son downstairs to go get the mattress. But he doesn't - he stays upstairs with me, so I have no choice but to apply these black straps to the bed as he watches.

When I glance over, his eyes widen, but he stays silent. He hears his son pushing the mattress up the steps, so he goes to assist while I perfect the placement of my naughty device. As they remove the plastic from the brand new plush mattress, the son asks his papá what I'm doing in Spanish.

"No es importante, Mijo," he says while shaking his head.

The salesman told me the delivery men would be Spanish-speaking, so I probably should have had my neighbor Gabriel or even Diego come over. Though we all know how *that* would have ended. New vibrating bed? Sex restraints? Diego probably wouldn't have even waited for the men to leave before ravaging me.

The son tries to press the matter because it appears as though he wants an answer, but his father nervously mutters in Spanish something close to, "don't worry about it and work." My Spanish is still nowhere close to perfect, so I can only pick out certain words when native speakers are conversing quickly.

He is a very handsome young man, so, sorry to tell you Pops, but one day I think he *will* find these black straps to be important. But in the meantime, I'm so sorry that this is something you'll have to discuss with your child in the truck as you drive to your next delivery.

I tip them $20 and try to wipe the child corruption that just happened from my mind. What's done is done.

Add to my TO-DO list: Take this vibrating cruise ship on her maiden voyage

CHAPTER 5
supervised visitation

Now that my bedroom has been put back together post-delivery, I'm scheduled to go see my sister, Neka, today for a gathering she's hosting at her home. Leave it to her to be the most ghetto fabulous chick alive who stays living in the whitest possible neighborhood. The last time we all attended a gathering at her place, we collectively vowed that it would be the last time!

Her Labor Day cookout was a blast. Neka is a phenomenal cook and her man is fire on the grill. So when she sounds the alarm that she's hosting, we are all coming! About fifteen of her closest friends and family were gathered outside, eating, drinking, and playing spades, so all was going perfectly well until the kids came downstairs to get drinks and snacks. Then, out of pure habit, my niece locked the screen door behind her, unbeknownst to *any* of us! *All* of the adults were locked out, and for over four hours, those kids (ages four through eight) did not show their funky little faces! We were pounding on all the doors and windows, screaming their names to get their attention. No one could leave because our purses and keys were in the house. So I called OnStar to unlock my car to get a paper clip to try to pick her lock. But this woman had paid a fortune for her security doors and alarm system, so if I was able to pick that lock with a paper clip, she would've had everyone in Lowe's Windows & Doors department in line to be stoned to death.

Then someone got the bright idea to climb a ladder to try to open the bathroom window or at least try to get the kids' attention. Mind you, when a dozen Black folks are simultaneously pounding on *all* of the doors and windows in the not-so-Black neighborhood, that tends to concern the neighbors who, in turn, are likely to call the cops. Fortunately, no police came, but by the time 9pm did, there was no outdoor lighting because the switch was *inside*. There were also no bathroom privileges, and it had been hours!

Finally, the four-year-old came down to get a drink and stopped dead in his tracks when he saw a crowd of crazy people desperately banging on the door. Confused, he slowly came over to unlock it and everyone cheered and hugged him – then promptly lined up at the two bathrooms. The rest of the kids came down, and we learned that these little assholes were all upstairs with the door shut using the karaoke machine to play American Idol! I told Neka I was not coming back for another outdoor event until she got a hide-a-key for her Fort Knox house! Fortunately, the gathering today is inside.

"Heyyy sis," Neka shouts dramatically as she runs over to embrace me. "Why you so damn late? You ain't never late! Hell, I be tellin' you the wrong time so you won't show up early."

Sigh... this bitch got jokes.

"Well I woulda been early, but a lady stopped me while I was driving and asked me which way I was going because she needed a ride to the next town over."

"Oh, so you dropped your neighbor off somewhere? That's nice."

"Absolutely not. I had no idea who this woman was. I don't watch the news often, but I know enough not to let strangers in my car. So when I politely informed her that I was unable to comply with the request because I don't *know* her, this chick inserted her dusty ass arm into my vehicle to shake my hand and introduce herself like that was supposed to change something."

"Oh so *now* you know her, so you can take her where she needs to go?"

"Right!? So I kindly let her know that the bus stop was right over yonder and would probably be arriving in about the next twenty minutes or so."

"You be so damn proper," she laughs. "I bet you said that shit to her just like that, didn't you?"

"I mean, maybe a little," I laugh. "I don't wanna be rude."

"Wait, I thought you was bringin' Diego?" she asks, looking toward the door. "What happened?"

"I was planning to, but I haven't spoken to him. He's mad cuz when we talked and he was bringin' up my *past* situationships, he learned I'd slept with Will. It wasn't a secret. Unlike him, I have nothing to lie about. If you ask a question, I'll give you an *honest and immediate* answer."

"So the fuck what? They don't even *know* each other, plus you and Diego ain't even together anyway."

"Right!? And that was *way* before Diego," I reply. "It's not like Will pulled out and Diego instantly pulled in."

"Wait, ain't Will the one you were watching porn *alone* in your car so you could get hot enough to have sex with him cuz he didn't turn you on?"

"Biiitch! Yess! I even *told* Diego that, but he said I get too wet so he didn't believe me."

"Duh, cuz *you* turn her *on*, stupid!" Neka laughs. "Swear, men just be dumb."

"Exactly. So I don't know where he's at. He always makes up in his mind some ridiculous reason to just stop talking to me, which is why I wasn't trying to involve myself sexually with him. Oooops."

Neka laughs, "Well I hope it was at least a good 'ooops.' Hey what about dude out there on the porch with *my* deadbeat ass man? He got a nice body."

"Oh, you mean the one with the amazing biceps who just happens to be smoking a blunt the size of a paper towel roll?"

He sees us peeking out the window and holds up the blunt as if to ask, *y'all wanna hit this?* I'm steadily shaking my head no while Neka has an enormous ass smile on her face, nodding yes. I can't with her.

I'm still trying to figure out why every man who wants to date me can't survive without a daily dose of marijuana. Neka gave me a basic joint once, and I was so high I swore it was laced with something because it felt like I was having a stroke. So I haven't puffed since.

Really, I prefer a non-smoking man as well. A good many friends have called me picky over the years, but at my age, I'm just at a point where there are so many things that just are not attractive to me.

I recently spoke to a gentleman who told me that he smokes weed occasionally. I thought ok, a lot of people smoke weed occasionally. Hell, I used to visit the family and if the blunt was coming past, I'd hit it twice and keep it moving. But that was the extent of my drug usage for the month. I could leave and still pass a drug test. So out of curiosity, I asked, "How often is occasionally?"

"Every day," he admitted casually.

Hmmm... ok. So I brush my teeth *every day,* and I would never tell Dr. Dornin that I *occasionally* brush my teeth. Those two time frames aren't synonymous.

"Well how much are you smoking daily?"

"Oh, just two."

So I'm thinking, ok, you hit it twice a day, like two general puffs a day? Nooo, two blunts – two *whole* blunts a day! This man was rolling sixty blunts a month! How much does that cost!? I feel like I could pay a significant amount of my mortgage down with just the amount of money he was spending on weed!

So I gotta ask, because why not? "Where are you smoking all of this?" Because that's a lot of weed to me.

"In my apartment," he replied, as though that's totally normal.

"In your *one-bedroom* apartment?" Ok, it's gonna be a very hard sell to tell me that this man's *everything* – clothes, socks, boxers, whole apartment – does not smell like an entire weed factory! I once walked through my house with a Black & Mild cigar and I could smell that shit for the next four hours. So everything in his apartment just *has* to stink.

I sensed that *he* sensed I wasn't really ok with where this conversation was going – like at all. That much weed is just one of my deal breakers.

"It's ok because when we buy our home together we can have a room for that," he reassured, like that's the most perfect idea he'd ever had in his life.

Most people would delight in adding an exercise area or an entertainment room for the kids, or possibly even an office. Nope. This man had *weed room* on our list of criteria for our future home. Any guesses as to what's *not* about to be in my next home? Go ahead, just start throwing them out. Yeah, because you only need one guess. *Weed room*! Maybe that's for some people, just not quite for me. Personally, I would prefer one of those sound proof, erotic, blood-red sex rooms with all the kinky fun stuff. I get a little loud about it, so why not insulate the noise and keep everybody happy? But no, this joker's fantasy was a weed room.

I know there are men out there who can wake up and not need marijuana for breakfast. They exist, so can I just have one of *those,* please?

♀ ♂ ♀ ♂

I always leave my sister's house with an over-abundance of food since she always cooks to feed double the amount of people in attendance. So, after stuffing my fridge with the leftovers, I get comfy and prepare for my nightly porch ritual. It's fire time. This is my peace and my solitude, sitting on my porch with a crackling fire and lately a good book. I could literally do this for hours.

Just as I am about to learn who murdered this fictional man's mistress in my new Jeneva Rose novel, I hear a deep voice call to me from the street. I avert my attention from the book to the presumably chocolate man in the large champagne-colored SUV.

"You lookin' real cozy on that porch right now," he shouts.

"Yeah, I try!"

"Would you mind if I come to join you?"

"Uhhh, sure?"

Ok so this is either the best or worst mistake I have ever made in my entire life. Best-case scenario: he looks as good as he sounds, because I definitely can't see him in the dark inside of his car. Worst-case scenario: he's a total serial killer, at which point I will have at least captured his image on my ring doorbell when he approaches my porch.

As he drives around the block to park this mammoth SUV, I text my mother to let her know that a strange man has pulled up and is coming onto the porch and if she never hears from me again, have the detectives check the doorbell camera. Of course she replies, freaking out.

The champagne behemoth pulls up, and the gentleman exits the vehicle. As he approaches my porch, he smiles and all I see are his beautiful white teeth – all in a row! It's sad that these are things I get excited about these days. The handsome, clean cut gentleman introduces himself as Kelvin and I offer him a seat on the other side of the fire table. His dark brown eyes are very friendly, and as an added bonus, he smells amazing. So if he *does* murder me and his scent ends up on me, he will be very easy to track with one of those crime scene dogs.

Kelvin informs me that he has passed by my house many times and observed me relaxing by the fire, but has always been hesitant to say anything. We talk for a long while, then as kindly as he came, he left. *Well, if I never see him again, at least we had a nice, normal conversation. That so rarely happens lately.*

Add to my TO-DO list: Start bringing my mace outside just in case the next random visitor isn't so normal

CHAPTER 6
pandemic possibilities

What the hell is coronavirus? I can't front; I'm feeling some type of way about this one. I could barely date right when there *wasn't* a deadly virus spreading throughout the world. How am I supposed to find a man now? And I'm having trouble wrapping my mind around the fact that the last time I went out for anything fun *was* the last time – at least for a while. Had I known, I wouldn't have taken it for granted.

Then there's my mother, who is losing her ever-loving mind! In the midst of a global pandemic, all she can talk about is, "I CAN'T BELIEVE I MISSED THE LIQUOR STORE CLOSING!!" Texting me all crazy:

Mom: What am I supposed to drink?

Me: WAAATERRRRR!!!

Mom: I need something with some flava

Meanwhile, she only drinks *one* kind of alcoholic beverage – out here talkin' like she can hang with *real* drinkers.

Brie is on her way over and though my house is large enough that we can easily socially distance, the plan is to spend most of our time outdoors on the porch. But just in case, I crack all the windows to maintain good airflow through the house. It's a little habit I picked up when, for about six years annually, my mother would come home for Thanksgiving deathly ill. I told her to stop hugging people and eating at those potlucks at work, but she's like a giant child who refuses to listen. So I would make her wear a mask in my house. She thought that was the worst thing I could ever do to her, and that I was being completely irrational. Even though it was freezing out, I would crack all the windows so her germs weren't lying stagnant in my house and they had somewhere to go. She would be so angry, but guess what? She shouldn't have brought her sick ass to my house. Despite her annual contagious visits and working in tight quarters with five other breathing people, in the past nine years I have not had as much as a single cold. Knock on wood.

As Brie pulls up in her car with the music bumpin', I'm already out on the porch with my Clorox wipes disinfecting the chairs, preparing for a nice germ-free visit. This chick hops out of her car with a duffel bag and two bottles of wine and I begin to wonder if I agreed to some shit I didn't know I agreed to. *Like, is she staying here or something?*

And who drinks that much wine? I'm doing good to get through one glass. But regardless, I'm tickled to see her because it's been a long while since we've gotten to hang out. She runs up onto the porch and we're about to hug, but then we're not sure if we should because of the contagion. So we stand awkwardly staring at each other like, are we hugging or fist bumping or nodding or what?

"This is dumb!" and she just grabs me and gives me a big squeeze. I absolutely squeeze back because who knows when the next time I will get any physical contact.

While I am examining the bottles of wine to see if my picky self will be drinking any of it, Brie begins to squint as she looks just past me. "What the fuck?"

Brie immediately turns to run in the house and I follow with the wine in hand because Black People Rule 18, Section 4, Article B clearly states *when one sees a person of color randomly take off running, you run too! One does not need to know why the initial runner darted. We'll find out when we get there. Where is there? We don't know, but if she runs, then we gotta go too, because some shit is about to pop off.* I have relayed and repeated the rule to all of my Caucasian friends, so if they ever see me take off, they know what to do! These heifers know I don't just run for kicksies. Either I'm about to die, something is chasing me, or there are donuts somewhere. So when Brie runs, I run.

Come to find out, an insanely large animal was charging across the street toward us. So much for a porch visit. Brie's duffel bag is still outside and it will remain there until she leaves – or until that creature makes off with it, because I'm not going back out for it.

"Whose beast was that?" She says, panting.

I'm panting even harder because I'm in worse shape than she is. "My irresponsible ass neighbor down the street. That giant bull mastiff has attacked every one of my neighbors' smaller dogs!"

"Ok, well shit! We were almost on the menu! After that mini workout, I definitely need a drink. Get my heart rate back down."

Brie goes into the kitchen, washes her hands, grabs glasses, and begins to open the wine. I promptly hand her a Clorox wipe for the bottle. She shoots me a smart ass look, "So I bet that dumb bitch in HR feels real extra stupid now for reprimanding you for washing your hands and sanitizing your workstation." She jokes, "You were light years ahead of this pandemic!"

"Girl, right!? I have *so* many words for her simple ass right now!"

Brie wipes and opens the bottle. "So how is Docta Bae?"

"Who?"

"You know, your hot therapist."

"Shouldn't you be asking me how *I* am? And we're calling him Dr. Bae now?" *When did that happen?*

"Bitch, I hear about you all the time. I'm trying to hear about some *him*. And yasss hunny, it's Docta *Bae*."

Makes total sense. As I fill her in on how he's throwin' the Morris Chestnut vibes, I flip on the light above the sink and it pops so loudly that we both jump into each other's arms, spilling some wine. So much for all that social distancing. We're both getting "tha 'rona."

Brie is yelling at me to hurry and pull the plugs from the outlet because it's smoking and there is a distinct burning smell in the air. I don't want to go over there, though, because what if we blow up? Brie is a total soldier about it, so she goes over and unplugs everything while I venture downstairs to be sure the breaker is off for that portion of the kitchen.

It's always something. No one tells you when you buy a home, it's just going to constantly cost money. If something isn't breaking, it's flooding, if it's not flooding, it's leaking, if it's not leaking, it's making some weird noise. Fortunately, I have a very handy friend who is always down to help. I feel bad calling him because I know he absolutely hates my house. He liked it when he came to just see it, but the very first time he came to do any work was when I needed the locks changed.

I was able to use the circular drill to expand the size of the bedroom door knobs so they would look nicer, but for whatever reason, my doors on the outside were absolutely ridiculous. I used the circular drill, and it broke. So I went to get another one, and it broke as well. That's when *I* finally broke down and called Xavier because I had already torn half the door apart and drilled it to be damned, so the door had to get fixed before nightfall. He came down with a drill that was way more powerful than my little girly drill. This large muscular man could barely get the holes drilled through this door. And the whole time he was here, all he kept asking me was, "Whaaat the fuck are these doors made of? They have to be made with the same wood that Noah used to build his Ark! If I can't get in this door with a fucking drill, the robbers don't have a chance. Just let it go!"

We then broke yet *another* drill head but plus side, he finally got it fixed and the entire house smelled like Christmas from him destroying my pine door.

Since Xavier lives just up the street from me, he's kind enough to swing by on his way to the bar.

Glad I'm getting him before the alcohol because somehow liquor and electricity probably don't mix well.

Brie raises an eyebrow and tilts her head when the door swings open and a tall, light-skinned, muscular figure enters the living room. Not sure why every man I know has arms that look like two baby pigs fighting to escape a pillowcase. I guess I'm just blessed like that.

I hop up to offer a quick church-lady hug. "Brie, this is X, well... Xavier."

He nods at her with a smile while he tucks his unopened Black & Mild cigar behind his ear and removes his Timb's since I was out of shoe covers. Hell, they wouldn't fit his big ol' feet anyway.

"Nice to meet you," he says warmly as he strolls into the kitchen that almost exploded earlier.

Brie hops up from her seat with her wine in hand to watch him walk away with his large tool bag draped over his even larger shoulder. "Mmmm, more like triple X," she mutters under her breath.

"Stop it. That man is damn near married," I scold.

"So am *I*, shit! I'm just lookin', damn." And no one could blame her either. His distressed jeans and plain white tee tautly hugging his vast muscular physique, paired with a freshly shaven bald head, and green eyes that make you wonder who his daddy is? We *all* just wanna look.

"What the hell did y'all do to this outlet?"

Brie quickly chimes in, "Hell if I know. But if you're gonna come back to fix it, we're gonna do it again to every other outlet in the house."

He laughs while gesturing for me to go turn off the main power, but it's already off, so he begins working his magic.

After a number of attempts on his end and way too many trips up and down to the electrical box in the basement, Xavier is becoming increasingly frustrated because the outlet and light still aren't working and by now, they should be.

With wires re-exposed for about the fourth time, hanging out of my wall, "I don't know what the fuck!? I hate your house!" he snaps, slamming a screwdriver onto my granite counter.

"Now look, you break the counter, you're fixing that too! Maybe you're being too ginger. Just shove it all in there and see what happens!"

"Hello!" Brie says, raising her glass making my statement appear way dirtier than it was actually intended.

Xavier shoots me a look like I'm being an asshole and begins to sarcastically vent while theatrically shoving all the wires back into the wall with little regard. "I've been doing this for twenty years and you think... ya know what? Fine. Gonna just shove 'em all in here. Don't even matter. Whatever."

I run back down to the basement to flip the switch, kind of in vain because I *was* just being a smartass.

"Oh shit!" Brie screams.

I run back upstairs to find the light on, so I start doing my happy dance. "OMG, it worked! I'm a genius! I'mma switch professions tomorrow!"

Brie laughs while X stands there leaning against my counter with his arms crossed, shaking his head in disbelief.

"Makes *no* sense. Can I use your bathroom before I go? Your house makes my nerves bad."

"You're so dramatic. Sure."

Xavier runs upstairs, but I don't hear the door shut. *Please don't let this man just start peeing in my house with the door all open.*

"Yo why do you have all these ball caps with matching scarves?"

Brie and I exchange confused looks. *Ball caps? WTF is he talking about?* I definitely lay out all my clothes, accessories and shoes for the entire week on the banister just outside of my bedroom. And it's all been there since the pandemic because I am too lazy to put it all back since I began working remotely. But there are surely no baseball caps up there. So we run up to see what he's talking about.

When I flip on the hall light, he realizes those "ball caps" are actually a row of the largest bras ever made, of course, with matching panties underneath. FYI, those panties are nowhere *near* the size of scarves.

Xavier's eyes widen and his mouth falls open. "OMG, those are not ball caps," he says, turning off the light, then staggering into the bathroom and closing the door.

"Yo, I expect those to be put away by the time I come out of here!"

"Will do!" Brie says tipsily as she takes the molded fuchsia bra, plops it on her head, and enters my boudoir with her third glass of vino.

"Where does this massive structure live? And what size is this thing anyway!? We really could make matching ball caps with all this material."

"Wow you dusty roach, really? My *bra* lives in the third drawer and it's a 38H if you must know."

"Daaamn!" we hear shouted from the bathroom from this man who is clearly eavesdropping on our conversation when he *should* be emptying his janky ass bladder.

She stands in silence staring at me, then polishes off her wine, thoroughly increasing her tipsiness. "Lies detected. That's not a bra size, it's a parking level. I parked there on my last business trip."

She places the "structure," as she calls it, into the drawer and goes downstairs to refill her glass, leaving me alone to question my choice in friends.

♀ ♂ ♀ ♂

It's the height of covid season where we don't really know what's going on with this virus but we're supposed to be social distancing and wearing masks. I'm all good because I try not to get too close to anyone anyway and the people who *do* visit my porch easily distance, as the area is about twenty feet wide. But none of that matters when I decide to take my garbage out and recognize the ancient Chinese man who happens to be walking past my house. He used to come all the way out to where I work to use the computers in the library, even though we have a perfectly good library two blocks from where we're currently situated.

He recognizes me and approaches excitedly, speaking in very broken English. He's difficult to understand, but I can make out that he's 90 years old, from China, and that he walks every day all through the town to stay in shape. This is admirable because I don't want to walk from one room to the other in my house, let alone all over town. So this man is definitely *old people workout goals.*

With the heaviest accent you can imagine, he offers me a bracelet that he made by hand. It resembles something that a teenage girl would make with the colorful string and beads. I respectfully decline because well, covid... and I'm not really into jewelry. My matching Tiffany choker and bracelet with silver hoop earrings are the extent of my jewelry wearing.

He insists and begins to put the bracelet on my wrist, so we are now no longer six feet apart in the middle of a deadly pandemic. He begins to rub my arm while saying a Chinese prayer over the bracelet as I look and listen, wondering what he's actually praying for. He says it's for luck and that I will have good fortune. So I'm content with that, thank him and begin to try to add distance between us, but he is still holding onto my arm *and* my hand now because I guess he's not done yet. This ancient Chinese man, in the middle of covid season, begins to *blow* his breath – his potentially contagious air – up and down my arm after saying this prayer. All I can do is watch in abject horror because I can envision the covid developing on my dainty arm. I really just need to start being way ruder to people because this is a lot. But stupid here just stands and *lets* this stranger blow on me.

Upon completion of his ritual, I immediately go in and do a full surgical scrub of my entire arm, hoping that I didn't wash away his luck prayers on the bracelet. The cat just stares.

♀ ♂ ♀ ♂

Tonight I will binge Vampire Diaries and snack on my fave, Skinny Pop. As darkness falls, it gets eerily quiet on my street, thus watching spooky shows probably isn't the brightest idea. So naturally, I jump when I hear a car horn.

"Mind if I visit for a bit?"

It's Kelvin. I nod affirmatively as he parks the vehicle. I pause my show, offer him a drink, and we begin our chit chat by the fire. He's so handsome, it's such a shame. The more I get to know him, the more I'm learning that he has some deep-seated issues with women and to let him tell it, none of us are really trustworthy. We say we want a good man, but when there's one around, we don't know how to act. He wants to romance a woman, wine her, dine her and treat her like a queen, but he maintains that's not what we want. We desire the opposite of that and he doesn't seem to understand why women don't want to date him.

It quite literally goes on and on... and on. I get to hear about how women are primarily concerned about his profession. Well, the very first time we met, he told me what his profession was, so maybe don't lead with that and they could get to know him without judgement of his occupation. But that's just me thinking out loud with a very reasonable, rational solution.

You know me, I'm all about a good therapist, so I ask if he has sought therapy, considering he still seems very jaded from his impending divorce. He politely informs me he had a male therapist first, then a female, but was fired by this last one. I ask if it had anything to do with his views toward women and he replies that he's pretty sure it did. When a therapist, who usually isn't that cheap, declines your money because she either feels like you are that far beyond repair or is tired of being offended by the trash coming out of your mouth? That shit is like a bad football game where every referee walks onto the field and throws flags – except they throw giant red ones.

"So your therapist, like, fired you?"

"I mean, essentially yeah, I guess."

"You don't see this as a problem?"

"I mean, probably?"

Probably? This very handsome man then requests to ask me a question because he wants to get some honest feedback about a woman's thought process where he's concerned. I agree to answer this question and begin to listen to him talk, waiting for the query to be posed. This man talks about *everything.* For a solid seven and a half minutes, he goes on about Destiny's Child and how they could have still been amazing if they would have stayed together, that it's all Beyonce's fault, cars, travel arrangements, funerals, I feel like the Disney Store might have been mentioned in there somewhere, weather, clothing and shoes. Pick a topic out of the sky and this man has brought it up in these seven minutes of *straight talking* as I patiently listen to what's being said, just waiting for the connection and the actual question.

So finally, I interject softly, "Hey, I need to stop you right quick. What is the actual question?"

Somewhere, not sure where exactly, this man develops the audacity to stare at me in silence and respond with, "You are so insensitive!"

WTF!? I am not sure when trying to get to the point turned into me being insensitive. He said he had a question, and I sat and listened calmly and quietly for way too many minutes with him still never getting to the actual question or even to what the topic of the question would be. So I call my mother once he leaves to tell her this ridiculously insane story.

"Well, what was the question?"

"He never asked it," I state, blankly.

"Well damn, so did you refer him to your therapist? How's that going anyway?" she asks.

"Absolutely not! He would probably hunt me down and shank me if I sent this guy over there," I jest. "But it's goin' fine."

"That must mean Dr. McTasty is still smokin' up your computer screen?"

"OMG! What the hell is wrong with all of you? He's not even a doctor!"

"That is so irrelevant right now," she replies. "A shame he doesn't have a brother or something, a cousin? Young daddy? Or hell, an *old* daddy for *me*!"

"Oh, come to find out, there are like seven brothers! I know he can't actually hook me up with one of them because I'm sure that's a huge conflict of interest, but at the very least, point a bitch in the right direction where I could find one! Like 'brother A' will be at X Mall around 4:30pm."

"I know, right? Because it's not like he's treating you because you're actually crazy or something."

"Exactly."

"Hmmm..." then silence takes over the phone, which is weird for my mother. "Sooo, do lobsters have sex?"

What the actual shit is happening here? I cannot. Where did this randomness come from? What is on this old ass mind of hers that this is a question she feels compelled to arbitrarily ask me?

"I'm hanging up now. I will talk to you later when you have a more normal thought process. Love you."

Add to my TO-DO list: Register for some counseling courses right quick so I can officially charge *both* of these people $112/hour

CHAPTER 7
he ain't nothin' but...

Afuckboy. A pure, unadulterated fuckboy with stellar conversation skills. That's the version that I always inevitably end up getting from Diego. One would think that at his age, he would want to behave like a normal adult male, but alas, that would be too much to ask. It always seems like it may go differently, but the end result is always fuckboy status. And he mysteriously disappears from my life as quickly as he enters it, finding some way to blame *me* for said departure. This time it was, "I was mad because there was a man coming to your house." That is the most laughable excuse ever because, hey genius, the only man coming to my house was YOU – unannounced on every occasion, so if I were trying to date anyone else, that would have turned into a pretty awkward and probably volatile scenario.

Of course, Tyce still swings by to hang out, but he can't seriously still be mad about that because Diego is *not* actually my man and Tyce and I have been friends for twenty-four years.

That's over two decades of Diego experiencing a childish male pettiness towards another human that he's never even met in person. Mainly because he actually sat on my porch one day and told me he would fight Tyce. Seriously, are we in kindergarten? And for what reason would you want to throw hands with a man whose hands aren't even on *me*? Tyce could run any man down with his new luxury vehicle, crazy suit game, and pristine credit. He wouldn't need to throw a single punch. And considering he's been a more solid friend to me than most, including Diego, he isn't going anywhere. Hell, he's in the process of refinancing my house right now. So it's probably time to lose the anger and jealousy. I would say something crazy like, "*hey we're just hanging out on the porch; what could possibly happen out there?*" But we already know what goes down on the porch.

And here we are yet again, another woman that Diego is now mysteriously engaged to just months after suddenly disappearing from my life. It's not enough to just have a girlfriend after he ghosts me. He goes to get whole ass engaged – both times, which puts his ghosting status on a new level. All those trust issues I had with him, validated. My initial hesitancy to go further physically with him, validated. There is no way that he was not seeing us both at the same time, all while claiming there was no one else and being all hugged up with me in my kitchen saying crazy shit like, "let's have a baby." So what would happen? I would be bearing your child while you're walking down the aisle with another woman? I'm so glad I had the good sense and solid wherewithal to decline *that* foolishness.

I would regularly mention to him, "If you're not *asking me* for it, you're getting it from somewhere else." He would always reply with some form of, "that's not true," but I'm not stupid enough to buy that – I can't afford it!

All the quality time that I wanted with him, he was clearly giving to some other woman. And it's really cute, because she has so many wonderful things to say about him on social media, particularly involving loyalty. It's laughable considering he was in my inbox talking to me and never once alluded to the fact that he was in a serious relationship. Also, for him to become engaged that quickly, he had to have been dating her while he had me tied up with his mouth wrapped around my entire tootsie pop, making me scream like a banshee.

So while I now give you permission to call me Princess Petty, I hope she enjoyed the way my juice box tasted every single time she kissed him. That man rarely left my house without putting his lips on every single one of mine.

DING DING

Diego: U need ur car washed?

Renée: Probably but I can do it

Diego: I'm comin' over

Damn, he's stubborn. Diego pulled up in his ever so pristine Charger, which he has detailed weekly whether it needs it or not. He and an older Black gentleman exited the vehicle as he gave me that sly smirk for which he's famous. After informing me that he had brought this man here to detail my new SUV, he whispered in my ear, "and while he's wettin' up ya car, I'ma be wettin' up..." then boldly stared into my eyes while he ran his fingertips up my inner thigh toward my special lady gift that was definitely ready to be unwrapped.

The awkward look on that poor older man's face as he stood nearby visibly matched his perceived discomfort. He had to be over sixty-five years old – that's like getting nasty in front of a father figure. However, since my paternal unit was trash, that didn't stop my freaky behind from becoming instantly aroused. But there's no way he would leave this man out here alone to go pleasure me.

Lies. After getting the detail man set up and grabbing him an ice-cold bottled water from the fridge, I was hoisted up over a muscular shoulder and carried over to the bottom of my steps. This is no easy feat, as I'm a pretty sturdy chick. Still not sure how he managed to set me down while expertly sliding down my shorts and lace panties simultaneously. As he went in for the kill, he was momentarily paused when his forehead met the palm of my hand with a smack.

"Dude, you can't for real think this is ok. That man is *right* outside! He will hear *all* of this!"

I was given a look of, "that's not my problem, let him hear it" as he grabbed and restrained the arm that initially blocked him and proceeded to his intended destination. He had zero regard for the fact that my stairs are situated a mere few feet from the *open* front door, where anyone passing by on my heavily traveled street would be able to see and hear anything taking place.

Mini moans escaped me as he paid his regular visit to the twins, but as his active tongue and ravenous mouth made their way further south, things became way more audible! I tried my best to keep the volume down, but the way this man handles me... *SHIT!* The toe sucking, waist grabbing, thigh biting, ass smackin'... the effortless way he threw my legs over his shoulders so he could hold on to the front of my thighs, thus preventing my escape from his tongue tornado... all on the steps within less than four feet of space. This man was eating his lunch *so* good that, *damn, am I hearing bells!? This dude got me hearing actual bells!*

When I threw my head back in complete ecstasy, I saw my cat sitting two steps above. Great! So I wasn't hearing things – it was her collar bell. She sat watching in judgement as if to say, "Really bitch, *this* shit again!?"

I felt bad because we were blocking her egress down the stairs, but once I grabbed a fistful of plush carpet with one hand, the wooden baluster with the other and a series of hefty grunts and groans escaped me, she'd had enough and ran back upstairs right before I –

"OMG WHY WOULD YOU STOPPP!!??"

Lips glistening, Diego's head raised, and his gaze penetrated my soul as he smirked, then giggled. *He did that shit on purpose.* So naturally I did what any sane, frustrated woman would do to the smug prick who brings her to the precipice of unbridled pleasure, then stops. I started beating his ass and kicking my heels into his back while screaming obscenities that I didn't care if the world outside heard.

His silent strength is definitely scary sexy. He climbed the steps while crawling up my breathless body and whispered forebodingly into my ear, "Ohhhh.... Yeah. You gon pay for that."

Oh shit.

Before I knew it, I was once again scooped up, carried to the master suite and abruptly deposited onto my bed. This man wasted no time outstretching my limbs and tethering them securely to each restraint strap. His masterful work left me completely unable to shift even an inch. Diego opened my toy chest and, like a deranged serial killer methodically selecting torture devices, began to lay items neatly at the foot of my bed between my open, restrained legs. Blindfold. Nipple clamps. Riding crop. G-spot wand. In one hand he held a silver satin gag, in the other the black ball gag. I remained quiet, praying he selected the satin, my preferred gag. And I knew if I got mouthy, he would use the other, which *really* prevents me from talkin' shit. He stared at me pensively, then put the ball gag back in the chest and added the satin gag to his lineup. *Thank you!*

He offered me a sip of the bottled water that I keep on my nightstand, then I mentioned, "The window is open."

"I don't care," he countered as he placed the gag in my mouth and tied it firmly, since I escaped it last time. "You misbehaved on them steps back there. You know better," he reprimanded with his thick accent. "Now, I'm gon make you come until you cry."

Excuse me, what? His sadistic grin was the last thing my huge anxious eyes saw before they were covered by the blindfold. All hell broke loose in that bedroom, and if the whole neighborhood heard about it, well... I pay these taxes.

Diego's punk ass brought me to the brink of orgasm *three* times before finally allowing me to finish, after which I was completely delirious and devoid of functional thought. I don't know how many more times it happened after that first one. As I laid completely spent with my blindfold soaked in the orgasmic tears he'd promised, I felt him loosen my right arm restraint, then a kiss on the forehead, and on the stomach. Still gasping for breath to get more oxygen to my depleted brain, by the time I found the strength to lift the blindfold and undo my left arm, Diego was gone.

I laid there for a while, then it hit me. Covid. With a groan, I heaved myself up, then stumbled down the steps with weakened legs to find my phone so I could ask Google if you can get covid-19 from oral sex. The answer was no, thank goodness.

I guess it's a good thing I didn't kiss him goodbye because less than a week later, Diego called me to tell me he'd tested positive for Coronavirus. Thinking back, it all made sense because the day after that visit, he stopped by and looked a mess. Diego prides himself on his structured appearance, but what showed up at my door was a special breed of crazy. He was very lethargic and actually fell asleep on my couch, which never happens. We both just attributed it to the fact that he works nights, or at least he *said* he worked nights; he could have been with that other woman. Either way, I done told that man about runnin' these streets, but he didn't listen. Fortunately, I didn't contract it, so this was one of the few times the internet was correct.

Little did I know that would be one of the last times I saw Diego.

Every time I think back on that little adventure, it makes me wonder if he drove that older man to *her* house to wash *her* car next and put his questionable mouth all over *her*.

So who knows? He was able to show her a completely different side of himself than he ever elected to show me, so maybe it can actually work between them. Or maybe she just has lower standards and is okay with 90% of the things that I'm not. Though there have been two other failed engagements before this one, that I know of, so his track record with putting a ring on it is no indication that he'll *actually* be walking down the aisle. This one seems like she has it a little more together than the others, but only time will tell...

♀ ♂ ♀ ♂

I didn't think I would ever see Kelvin again after he called me insensitive and ran off, but surprisingly, he has returned with his long-winded self. And naturally, the conversations continue in the same manner about how women basically ain't shit, so I let him go on and ramble while I think of fun things like different types of cheese. I get pulled from my exhilarating thoughts of pepper jack when I hear this man say to me, "But you're the lady on the porch. You're supposed to have cookies and brownies and we're supposed to cry together."

"S'cuse me, what? Cry? With who?"

"With *you*!"

"About what?"

"All our problems."

What the actual fuck? Who signed up for that shit? And where did he get that I was supposed to have this endless supply of baked goods? I'm a woman with a full-time career and a part-time freelance business. When the hell does it look like I have time to just be baking pastries for kicks and giggles, especially for someone who just wants to spontaneously come by my house and eat through his emotions? Even when I feel like emotional eating, I find somewhere to *buy* the junk or I *order* my sweets from KC Cookies up the street. I am not Martha fucking Stewart.

"Yeeeah, so what I'm gonna need for you to do is hit up a bakery on your way to a new therapist, as I am unable to currently accommodate those particular requests."

See, now *that* would have been the time to call me insensitive because I don't have the mental fortitude to deal with this *and* exercise tact. At this point in my life, you get one or the other.

Add to my TO-DO list: Fill up my snack cabinet – for me, 'cause Kelvin's ass is stressing me *out*

CHAPTER 8
they're heeeeere...

Ariah absolutely detests phone conversation. I am convinced that if she ever has big news like an engagement to the fine ass man she's dating or bears her first child, I will absolutely get a surprise text about it. But she knows that I prefer phone conversations to texting, especially since covid. I would much rather catch up verbally and hear my friends' voices. Occasionally, I receive a phone call from her and she's usually really good about returning mine.

"So any plans for the 4th?" she asks.

"You know damn well ain't nobody celebrating 4th of July over here."

"Juneteenth," we both say simultaneously

"Yeah, so I am not doing a damn thing except probably cleaning this wretched house because it looks like the Wreck of the Hesperus!"

My mother used to say that so much, but I had no idea what it actually meant, and until about six weeks ago, I still didn't. So I finally Googled "Wreck of the Hesperus" to see what it was, how bad it was, and if my house really is that ghastly? And those three answers would be, it was a shipwreck, pretty bad, and *yes*!

"Girl, I know you're trippin' because your house is always clean. It's never been a mess, even when I just pop up with my key."

"Yeah, about that –"

She interrupts, "So if it's clean during a surprise visit, then it's probably not as bad as you're makin' it out to be."

And she's not lyin'. My house is almost always perfectly tidy because I live on a main road and friends just randomly stop over to visit with very little notice. But today is an entirely different story, and I'm not quite sure what happened. My upstairs is usually pretty spotless, however, right now it looks like I hired four housekeepers and none of those bitches came downstairs to work. So I quickly snap four photos of my downstairs and send them to Ariah while we are on the phone so she can see that I really am not making up this tragedy.

"OMG! What the actual shit is happenin' right now in your house? This ain't normal! Are you okay? Are you depressed?"

I *told* her it was a whole travesty. How does the dining room that is almost never in use end up with this much random mess everywhere? There are about four loads of clean laundry in baskets stacked up, waiting to be folded. As you gaze around the dining room, my standing workstation is in shambles because, well, I have no actual reason for that other than work stresses me the fuck out, so screw that workstation and everything on it! The cat has a corner with a basket of her toys, which are just strewn about because she plays with everything and doesn't put anything back, much like a toddler. My usually pristine living room needs vacuumed in six of the worst ways and there are clothes everywhere. Since the majority of the clean clothes are in the basket downstairs, if I need something, I just go downstairs to change... yes, in front of all the windows in this ginormous house! So to my neighbors who have seen all of my *special places*, my bad. I reiterate, *I* pay this mortgage so...

But I digress. Nothing has been dusted in weeks and a collection of empty cans and glasses linger on any hard, flat surface available. Why? There is no reason for me to be living in this type of squalor. And don't even get me started on my kitchen. My normally immaculate kitchen is like an especially frightening scene from hoarders. Dishes for *days*! The dirty ones are rinsed off but literally stacked up along the side of the refrigerator. I have no clean spoons or knives, and it had gotten to a point where I actually ate yogurt with a fork! I just didn't feel compelled to go buy plastic ware. I *should* just wash the stinkin' dishes. Shall we discuss how I have not mopped the floor in a month (and a half) of Sundays and the garbage that's just piling up? Thank heavens I have a cat who is not fazed by trash or old food and is really well behaved. Otherwise, that garbage would have been all over the kitchen. At one point during the week, I was cleaning out the refrigerator, but something distracted me and I stopped. I think it was the new episode of Law & Order SVU.

As Ariah and I continue to discuss how there's a special place in hell for me for letting my downstairs look like this, I notice a miniature car pull up outside of my house. It's fire engine red, so that can only be my mother. *Shit! Regina's here.* Didn't tell a soul, just showed up like she has bills in her name or something. And this house has never looked worse.

"Girl, I gotta go," I say hurriedly. "My mama just showed up!"

"Oh damn! What are you gonna do?"

"Put her to work, I guess! Shiiit, she showed up here so we 'bout to clean this house!"

"Even though you always say she's like a whole damn child and is gonna just mess it back up?" Ariah asks, making all the sense in the world.

"*Exactly*! So there's probably not even a point to cleaning. But she's gonna want a spoon at *some* point."

Ariah giggles and wishes me luck as we end our call. I go outside to greet my mother and help her unload the car. As much as I have lectured her about over-packing, because we don't usually go anywhere of importance when she's here, it doesn't matter. She still fills her car with luggage and it usually takes about three trips each to unload.

"Surprise!" she screams as she excitedly jumps out of the driver's side. "I took off a couple days and decided to come visit." *Ohhh, in the middle of a pandemic... great.* She runs over to give me a giant hug.

After multiple trips to and from the guestroom, along with hearing her mouth about the condition of my downstairs, she curtly informs me that my house is not in a suitable condition for her dining experience, so she's going to enjoy her takeout on the porch. She then shoots me a look that pretty much says, "clean your nasty house, heifer."

After only a few minutes outside, mama re-enters the house holding her food with an exasperated look on her face, shaking her head.

"You just basically told me my house looks like our garbage company mistook it for the local landfill. Why are you in so soon?"

She stares at me with a deadpan expression. "I'm done. A hearse just drove by."

I look at her in confusion. "Okayyy, well there are three funeral homes within a few blocks, soooo... that's pretty standard."

Mama breathes heavily and presses her hand to her heart. "There were two kayaks strapped to the top of the hearse. It's just too weird out there!" Then she grabs some paper towels from the kitchen and heads upstairs with her meal.

She ain't lyin'. Last night when I was sitting outside, this skinny white dude from the domestic disturbance apartments next door was outside in his undies and yelled at someone, "I'm not an asshole, I'm the WHOLE ASS!!" He also was getting arrested a few nights before that and swore to the police that his Wi-Fi was watching him. If we're being honest, he may not be too far off base with that one, but I will set my conspiracy theories to the side on that topic. Though it would've been funny if someone had hacked his Wi-Fi and changed the name to "watching you."

Last week, there was an interracial lesbian couple outside of my house arguing about who was more of an addict. The one said she's not because all she does is smoke weed. *WTF!? I thought I moved OUT of the hood!* Then two cop cars and one undercover showed up because it was so loud someone must've gotten tired and called. After some back and forth, the cops left, then someone drove up and handed the couple a bi-racial baby and they walked off hand-in-hand, presumably agreeing to disagree on the topic of who was the bigger addict.

But I guess that's not as bad as my friend's crazy neighbor who threatened to kill the mailman if he continued to... wait for it... deliver the mail. And then there's the man who was whole ass, booty butt naked, sitting on his porch in broad daylight smoking a joint with not a care in the world – like everything he was doing at that time in his life was totally legal and socially acceptable.

Add to my TO-DO list: Give this house *back* to the previous owner and RE. LO. CATE.

♀ ♂ ♀ ♂

Lying across the foot of the bed in the newly upgraded guest room, I'm chatting with my mother, who is pretty excited about the new additions – a mini fridge beside the bed, a 50-inch flat screen TV on the opposite wall, and the giant metal clock above the bed. Though I think that when she requested a clock in the bedroom, she meant a digital one she could look at and tell the time in the middle of the night. But I'm so extra, I went balls out and bought the giant structure to act as wall art to fill an otherwise empty space.

She peeks over my shoulder to see why my phone keeps jingling at half past midnight. My Ring doorbell keeps alerting me that someone is at the front entrance.

"Who is at your door at this hour?" She questions suspiciously.

"Probably just people walking by. The sensors reach out to the sidewalk," I explain as I open the app on my phone.

We begin to watch the recorded event on the screen, but there's no one there. We just see strange white fuzzies and flashes dancing about the porch area near the doorbell. So I back up to the previous event where the app claims there's "someone at the door," and more of the same. Just long wavy fuzzies that flicker near the doorbell camera.

We stare at each other in questionable disbelief because Black people never fare well in these situations in the movies.

"What. The hell. Is that?" I ask.

"I don't know, but if it keeps up, I got matches; we ride at dawn," she states dramatically, clearly indicating that we may have to burn this bitch down if the Spirits of the Damned plan on taking over the residence. We're not staying for that – y'all can *have* the house!

This isn't the first time we've encountered strangeness here. On the second day of move in, I was cleaning out one of the large open cubbies above the wide guest room closet, where I found a Ouija board! I didn't know what to do with it and I didn't want to touch it because again, in the movies, Black people get possessed and always die *first*. I don't need those problems; I just bought the damn house.

So naturally, I took to social media to find out what to do in this unbelievable situation. I got a ton of mixed comments; one as crazy as, "Take it out into the middle of the street and set fire to it." So yeah, as the new neighbor and the only person of color on this block, I would've looked totally sane setting fire to a board game in the middle of my heavily traveled street. The holdup of traffic alone would've had these people trying to cut me.

Someone told me to put the house back on the market, which I actually contemplated for a hot second, but I had already paid the painter, so that was out.

Another told me not to touch it with my bare hands and take it far away to leave in someone else's trash. So that's what I did – went downstairs, got the rubber gloves and like a total psychopath, I walked it at arm's length a block down the alley and left it in someone's trash can, resolute in the fact that, much like in the movies, if it showed back up the next day in the same place where I'd originally found it, I would throw the whole house away and start over.

Then I think about the cat. Is this why she hasn't come upstairs for the duration of my mother's visit? Did my mother bring the Spirits of the Damned *with* her? Usually every morning, the cat comes upstairs and goes into the guest room to visit with my mom. She'll sometimes bring her favorite stick or string up to play. However, this entire visit, we've seen neither hide nor hair of this cat. She has stayed in the farthest corner of the basement the entire five days my mother has been here.

I feel like animals sense things, so what the hell does she know, and why isn't she telling *us*? If something lies beneath, we want to know so we can get the hell out too!

The next morning, preparing to leave, my mother walks into the kitchen and gives me a big squeeze because we've always been a very affectionate pair. When she separates from me, she notices this cute little cylindrical silver and black device with a blue light shining brightly. She gets super excited and smiles really big!

"OMG! Tell her to do something! Alexa, start the car!"

I stare at my sweet naïve mother. "Ma, that's a Bluetooth speaker."

She looks over at me like I stole her puppy. It's just so sad that her daughter will never be technologically advanced. But it's ok, I'm not interested in Alexa. I don't want her listening to me; I say too much weird shit. She would be so traumatized by what she hears in this house, *she* would end up saying something like, "Alexa, return self to Amazon."

Once mama has left to go back home across state, I spend the rest of the day trying to coax the cat to finally come upstairs because none of this is normal. She's typically all up under me and following me everywhere, including to the bathroom.

I was once taking a pregnancy test, and she affectionately bumped my hand and I accidentally spilled the cup of hot pee all over her. She was *sooo* mad – just glaring at me in shock with her giant green eyes like, *you bitch, why did you just pour piss all over me?* I felt horrible but I couldn't stop laughing so hard, tears were streaming down my face as I snorted and hyperventilated! If there were ever a reason to hide in the basement, *that* should have been it!

Night falls, so I go back down to the basement to check on the cat, feed her, love her and clean her litter box. She's just lying on the floor at the bottom of the steps, peering up toward the kitchen. So I come over and look up too to see what the hell she's so intently focused on, then we hear a noise. We both flinch. She looks at me, I'm looking at her, and then we both dramatically return our attention back toward the kitchen.

I go live on Facebook because if the Spirits of the Damned *are* here and coming for me, this needs to be documented. I'm freaking out a bit because the cat can stay in the basement if she wants. All her food and everything is already down here. I, on the other hand, have to go upstairs at some point. We hear the noise again and the cat flashes a fearful glance at me like, *screw this! I'm out*, and she goes to hide in the back of the basement bathroom behind the curtain. This is why I need a damn dog. They don't abandon you – they're loyal, unlike fickle ass cats.

No sooner than I post my video saying that the Spirits of the Damned are in my house, I'm getting text messages from friends. No, let me clarify – my white friends. Because there is not a Black person alive who is going to text me in that situation, "Hey, need me to come over?" Not one. Our Horror Movie Heritage clearly dictates that we stay away from all things scary, supernatural, possessed, disturbed, ghostly, ghastly, ethereal, eerie, other-worldly, paranormal, mystical, etc... because we will not make it out alive. But in every horror movie, the white girl can trip, fall, roll down the hill in the middle of the woods and still make it out unpossessed and thriving, living her best life. So I'm guessing the film industry has given them this false sense of security, so they feel like they can offer to help out when the Spirits of the Damned have come to visit.

DING DING

Carrie: I'm on my way over

This bitch is crazy as hell! She tells me she's going to walk over to my house – it's the middle of the damn night. And she has a car – why is she not driving? But she says that it's a nice night, so she's going to walk the three blocks... across town... in the dark... alone... to aid me in combating the paranormal activity. So I grab a screwdriver that's in the basement tool kit, like that's going to help in this scenario, and stealthily slink up the stairs and dart outside to the porch to watch for Carrie.

Her short, thick frame is strolling down the street at 11pm, like no harm could ever come to her. She's wearing a short cotton dress, sandals, and carrying a big ass cup of wine, because I guess it only makes sense to bring wine to the exorcism?

While all of this is going on, I receive a Facebook message from Ella, my neighbor across the street. She's also volunteering her services to rid my home of the alleged apparitions within. Now that there are officially *two* white girls involved, it's inevitable that I will definitely die first tonight.

Ella is coming out of her house just as Carrie is about to stroll past it. She has her hands full, but I can't make out what's in them without my glasses. And I'm definitely not going back in for them.

The two crazy friends greet each other, then make their way over to my house, and Ella is *way* too chipper about this, skipping across the street. *This is good, maybe there is hope for me yet. The happy optimistic one also sometimes dies first in horror movies. This will give me time to escape.*

She approaches me with her clear blue eyes sparkling with excitement, holding a giant wooden object.

"Ella. What the hell is that?"

"You mean what the *heavens* is that? It's an Orthodox cross. It will protect us," she says, sounding more like Elle Woods from Legally Blonde than Ella, my normal neighbor.

"I brought the red wine!" Carrie says enthusiastically as she takes a swig of it from her insulated travel mug, already a tad tipsy.

"And here is some Holy Water," Ella boasts proudly, holding up a small glass jar.

"Where the fuck did you get Holy Water!?"

"Fuck and Holy in the same sentence!? Really, Renée?" Carrie chimes in. "No wonder your house is possessed." Then she takes another shot of vino.

"From the church," Ella says, like that's an obviously common occurrence. Look, to my knowledge, the Baptist church down the street ain't just giving out jars of Holy Water to its congregation.

"You *stole* Holy Water from a church!?" I shriek. "We're *all* going to hell!"

"Nooooo, I didn't *steal* it. They *give* it to us. *I'm* Orthodox," she says in a pretentious manner while flipping her shoulder-length blonde hair.

"What the hell does that even *mean*!?" I question, laughing and trying to comprehend the relevance of that in the middle of the night. "You know what, never mind. What do we *do* with it?"

"I'm not sure," she ponders. "I've only been possessed once... So are we goin' in?"

I wish I could see my *own* face! "HELL NAW you ain't bringing your demon-totin' ass in my house! That's all I need is you goin' in and accidentally leaving an *extra* one in there! Ain't nobody got time for that!"

Ella snickers and leaves the water with us, then goes across the street back to her sleeping child. Carrie fearlessly enters my Hell House, sprinkles the water all over, and even drips some on the cat, which I'm sure I'll hear about later. She stays for another hour or so and we engage in some girl chat so naughty, it would make all the poltergeists blush. *Good!*

For the time being, all is quiet, but I'm going to have a hell of a time convincing myself that it's safe to fall asleep again.

Add to my TO-DO list: Teach the Spirits of the Damned how to work this vacuum cleaner if they plan on staying

CHAPTER 9
yes, i'm black and it's my house

"**A**re you seriously *here* right now!?" I screech from my porch as Diana exits the cute burnt orange rental she just parked in front of my house. "Why didn't you tell me you were coming? I woulda sexied up for my princess Di," I laugh as we give a lengthy embrace, realizing too late that I'm not wearing my mask.

"I wanted it to be a surprise!"

"Well it *is*! Sit, sit! What can I get you to drink?"

"I know I just drove here, but a glass of wine would be great!"

"Dry red or sweet white?" I ask, so proud of myself for having impromptu options.

"Surprise me."

I opt to fill two giant decorative glasses with Bartenura Moscato d'Asti so I can drink and toast with my long-lost friend.

Diana and I met in grad school, sharing classes with Brie and Ariah. Similar to most of my friendships, we took a quick liking to each other, and we *all* shared a strong *dis*like for our college's program director who just so happened to reciprocate those feelings. We got the impression that he didn't seem to care for women *or* minorities and I aptly fall into both categories. To further solidify that impression, he failed me in his ethics class, citing that I was .25 points from receiving the "C" I needed to pass, as there are no "D's" in grad school. How convenient, considering he graded assignments and exams using only a letter system and never a point system. Fortunately, but to his disappointment, my other grades were strong enough to take that hit and *not* land me on academic probation. I re-took the class while he was on sabbatical, using the *same* notes and assignments from his semester, and got an A-. So clearly, the issue was with me and not my exceptional work.

Diana's loathing increased exponentially when this same director decided he wanted to go on vacation at the end of the summer and moved all of her class' assignments up by three weeks. He told them if they didn't submit all seven papers by the end of *that week*, they would fail the class. Of course, no one was able to meet that unreasonable deadline, so he kept his word and failed everyone! They were able to fight that, but our graduate schooling should not have been that traumatic. Though it definitely prepared us for real life. But I digress. I haven't seen her since she abandoned the

Steel City to live on the west coast to try something new.

"So, loving the hairrrrr," I sing to her as I deliver her glass.

Diana's long, thick, brunette hair had been chopped into an adorable pixie cut, noticeably emphasizing her bright blue eyes and flawless smile.

"Thaaanks," she sings back. "Hubby's not too sure about it. Nothing to pull on now."

"I mean, those *are* important factors to consider," I agree. "But it'll grow back, so in the meantime he'll have to find other areas to occupy those hands when he's feeling frisky."

We toast to that and let the drinking commence.

"So you're out on the west coast. Talk to me about how hubby *still* doesn't have a hot, single, chocolate man for me. I'm gonna die alone out here."

"Right!? I know! All of our chocolate, as you say, friends are married. Sorry girl. Are you still swiping?" she asks.

"I am, but these dating apps are getting soooo old! No one is normal and they all wanna do weird things with my feet," I say with a scrunched-up face. "I can't blame them, though. I do have beautiful feet that were *made* to be nibbled on, but that isn't a prerequisite."

"I know it's been forever since I last dated, but I feel like there has to be *one* normal one. Gimme your phone."

Diana puts her glass down and gestures for my cell. I unlock it and hand it over.

"Here, take it," I demand after opening the app. "Swipe for me and find me someone *you* think I would match well with. If he swipes for me too, then I promise I'll talk to him and you can be honorary matron of honor in the wedding."

"Cool! This should be fun!" she says excitedly.

It's so cute that she thinks that. Her optimism is adorable.

She begins thoughtfully man shopping. I sip on my wine and smile as she takes the time to read the profiles, because she knows that's what I would do before swiping right to match with anyone.

She must mean business because she positions the chair such that she's able to throw her long, slender legs up onto the ledge of the porch and fully commit herself to the process. I sense it's not going so well by her fidgeting, sighing, and facial expressions, but she remains silent as she attempts to complete this mission.

"Ok," she says in a serious tone. "I know why you're single. These men are all broken."

No shit.

"It's like every man on here is some kind of stereotype! I have never seen more penis grabbing, throwin' up gang signs, middle fingers *up*, pants saggin' *down*, face tats – like why do you need your area code permanently placed above your eyebrow? Are you going to forget it? And don't even get me started on the gold grilles, missing teeth, teeth on *top* of teeth, missing clothes, forty-year-olds dressed like twenty-year-old rappers... And can someone *please* explain to me how a profile says "doesn't smoke" but he's holding a cigarette in one pic and a blunt in another? I can't. I'm literally never leaving my husband," she rants in what sounds like one giant run-on sentence, then chugs the remainder of the glass.

Welcome to MY world. This chick is preachin' to the choir. I maybe swipe right once in every 120 profiles for all the reasons she listed and then some. Women look crazy all filtered, but to see men with snapchat filters? I can't. And the number of my friends' boyfriends, fiancés, and husbands on these dating sites and apps is getting excessive. Like, didn't I just swipe left on you on Bumble? Now here your ass is on Tinder talkin' about how you're looking for "something discreet." How discreet do you think it'll be when I tell your girl? Oh, because I'm tellin'! We have all these STD's to worry about and now covid!? If my man were out here runnin' these contagious ass streets trying to give *both* sets of my lips a virus, I would want to know!

My favorite was the bald, whole head and face tattoo guy who sent my very clean-cut self a message. This rather large gentleman had a facial skull tattooed on the top and sides of his head, adorned with skeletons, masks, bloody bullet wounds, stitches, bones, and upside-down crosses. One of the skeletons had the nerve to be wearing a cape pushing a wheelbarrow full of skulls.

Diana is skeptically frowning at me, like she doesn't believe such a person could exist. So naturally, I pull up the photo that I've saved because these people are like aliens and big foot – if you don't have photographic evidence, it didn't happen.

"Wowww, so he thought you'd make a nice match, huh?" She smirks.

"He thought wrong," I state as I get up to refill the drinks. I take Diana's glass in with me, but decide to just bring the bottle out instead because I'm certain this conversation won't be over for a while.

As I step back out onto the porch and begin to refill her glass, an older Caucasian gentleman with gray hair is slowly yet unsteadily approaching my home and looking up at us like he has some things to discuss.

Diana subtly whispers out the side of her mouth, "You know this dude? I got my dad's gun."

I giggle then whisper back, "Ummm, hold your heat, boo, probably not necessary. And no, he's not a neighbor."

I reclaim my seat across from my friend, who is still chillin' with her legs atop my ledge like this is *her* shit.

The gentleman, who looks to be easily in his eighties, finally makes it up the stairs and speaks to us. He looks to Diana and asks, "That vacant place next door, do you know who owns that?"

He's referencing the domestic disturbance apartment next door that is now available for rent. Diana turns her head and looks at me, so I respond that I have no idea because I think it was sold recently. He thanks me and looks back to Diana to ask, "Do you think they would allow pets?"

Diana again looks at me with a smirk, tilting her head dramatically. So I respond that I had never seen any tenants there with pets. He thanks me and *again*, looks back to Diana and asks, "How's the neighborhood here? Is it quiet?"

"Sir, I don't *live* here; *she* does."

He looks at my li'l chocolate face, so I smile at him as if to say, "surprise."

"Oh," he says nodding, still staring at me and looking around to observe my beautifully landscaped yard and well-decorated porch. "OH!"

I politely inform him that the neighborhood is, in fact, relatively quiet, but that the church bells go off at noon and six pm.

He thanks me and quickly leaves my property, presumably concerned that he would have Black neighbors? Who knows? But I get that sooo often since purchasing my home.

I was once cleaning my porch and asked by a random passerby what cleaning service I work for, because, "this residence always looks so good."

Thank you? But not the housekeeper – I'm the house owner.

I was cutting some of my hyacinths to enjoy in the house, when someone pulled up and asked why I was "cutting that lady's flowers" and threatened to call the police.

Ummm, I'm outside in white socks with a vase full of water and scissors – I AM that lady. These are my flowers, you dick.

The drunk homeless couple who hangs out all over town broke glass in the street, so I went out with a broom to sweep it up so none of the neighborhood dogs would get injured. A woman stopped at the stop sign and said to me, "Wow, you're sweeping the *street*? My housekeeper would *never* be *that* thorough."

Lady, I am not the housekeeper; I am the house OWNER. Literally gonna hang a sign on my property.

Alexis and I were once chillin' on the porch sipping on some frozen drinks, hers virgin, when an ADT sales representative approached. He greeted us, then proceeded to give an entire sales pitch... *to Lexi.* When he went in for the close, we smiled at each other as she informed him that she didn't own the house; I did. In his bewilderment, he became flustered and attempted to shift his pitch to me, but I was having no part of that. How about in the future, ask who owns the home instead of simply assuming? But I don't get many solicitors these days since adding my NO SOLICITING signage that states:

- We are too broke to subscribe to it

- We know for whom we're voting

- We have found the Lord and

- He hath provided a good security system

- We're even content with Comcast

- So unless you're selling girl scout cookies, candy, or hoagies, don't you *dare* ring that bell!

"Well no wonder you need therapy," Diana comments. "Speaking of which, I heard about Counselor Boo."

"Excuse me, counselor what? And from who?"

"From Brie, duh. So spill it."

I hate my friends. Diana spends a few more hours with me catching up after her request to try our town's famous Police Station Pizza! Of course she loved it, and it helped her sober up before her trek home.

Add to my TO-DO list: Hire a housekeeper, so maybe *then* I'll be viewed as the homeowner

♀ ♂ ♀ ♂

As I open my eyes, total darkness surrounds me. Annoyed, I glance over at the soft glow of the nightstand to see that it is 4:45am – on a Sunday. Naturally, my body would opt out of staying asleep and I would have to wake up to pee like a whole damn toddler. It is around this time every morning that I become super grateful for my new bed frame, whose remote has its own side of the bed and is always nearby. I hit the button that turns on lights beneath the bed, softly illuminating the floor so I can at least see while I stumble like a drunkard to the bathroom.

Ohhh, what the actual shit? I left my window open and because my neighbors in the apartments next door smoke outside, it smells like I sat in my bathtub and smoked a whole *meadow* of weed! If I spin around three times in here, I'd probably fail a drug test! Why do I even bother trying to escape it? At this rate, I might as well start growing it in my basement.

I sit on the toilet wondering if this shrunken bladder situation is my new normal and if I will ever again sleep through the night. As I'm completing my new bathroom ritual, my left arm vibrates to indicate that something's going on with my phone. One day I will actually get with the times and spend too much money on one of those fancy watches that has the whole internet on it.

I know that if I pick up my phone right now, I will be up for the rest of the morning and never get back to sleep. I'm able to resist for a good thirty seconds before giving in to see what's going on. Of course I would have two new matches. That damn Diana... this is *her* doing because I didn't swipe right for either of these.

The first profile reads:

Ladys, give the filters a break. some of us want to see what you actually look like.. im a boob guy btw.. Do you women watch the news, all you see is stuff about child trafficking so why do you post tons of kid pictures of a dating site? Wake up!!...what happened the the good ole 80's bush? lol.....

Seriously? How'd we go from grave concern regarding sex trafficking to the 80's bush? I know this tramp didn't for real swipe right on this dude. We're gonna need to have a chat! The second guy matched with me and left a message, to which I immediately replied because his profile seemed normal and he used punctuation. He's an oral surgeon. Not a fan of the dentist, but I would date one.

Dr. Man69: What are you looking for at this point in your life? Love? A relationship? Platonic friendship? A fuck buddy? Or what? And be honest Renée.

Me: I am looking for a relationship. There is too much out here to be sexing random ppl.

Dr. Man69: Listen to me, I'm looking for a serious and long term relationship. I want a woman who is honest a faithful submissive loyal freaky/kinky/open minded sexually affectionate has big tits a fat pussy can handle a Big Black Cock gives great blowjobs swallows is caring sweet and hardworking. Now, I'm all for getting to know a woman however I want a woman I can get to know as well as be intimate with. I've been single for the last 7 years. I'm a man and a man has needs. If I'm going to be having sex, it's going to be with someone I can just get dumb nasty with.

Wow. If that's what you're looking for in a woman, wonderful, but there is a better way to frame that than word vomiting every vulgar thing you can think of after a "nice to meet you."

I hate it here.

Add to my TO-DO list: Find out if mail-order husbands are a thing so I can delete these dating apps

CHAPTER 10
covid courtship

My phone jingles to let me know I have an online match. *Who the hell is this!?* Must be someone else Diana swiped right on. *But he only has one picture posted. Sigh...* everyone in the online dating world knows full well what it means when a man only has one photo up. That's the *best* picture he's ever taken in his entire life and in person (and any other photo ever taken), he looks like a damn boogawolf!

Tinder allows a dater to post up to nine pictures. From *my experiences*, when every photo is taken in a hat, something is wrong beneath it – bad hairline, misshapen head, extra-large forehead? When all nine photos are in sunglasses, I have an entire paycheck to bet that something is going on with one or both of his eyes or brows – missing eye, glass eye, words tattooed in place of brows, no eyebrows? When there are only headshots available, he is absolutely built like a potato. No other assumptions can be made. And lastly, when nine photos have no smiles, I promise there is some sort of dental failure

– there always is. Then there are those extreme cases where in every picture he's wearing a hat, shades, *and* not smiling. That's when I swipe left with haste because I have learned that it's about to be a whole mess.

The message reads:

You are so beautiful; I can't wait to have my lips pressed against yours.

Did no one tell this man we're in the middle of a pandemic? Though, I do miss physical affection. I haven't been kissed well in years, and covid isn't helping because I definitely don't want to put my mouth on or near anyone right now. So that's not going to help with the whole "me trying to find love" thing.

Even back in the day when I was looking for love, people were trying to get me hooked up. And when *he* came into my workplace, because he's Black and there were very few minorities there at the time, everyone was losing their minds. But I wasn't immediately attracted to Cole. He just wasn't my type – at all! Not to mention the fact that he was about eight years my junior and already had a girlfriend. But because we were the only melanin-enriched people in the building, we definitely ended up chatting and getting to know one another. He told me about his girlfriend and that she was in college locally. He was also in college but rarely got to see her. He was putting in the effort and wanting to spend time with her, but sadly, she wasn't reciprocating. So we just started hanging out more and more until, whoops, our lips fell onto each other's.

Let me talk to you about how this barely adult child was the most amazing kisser. I had never been, nor since have I been, kissed like that. Every embrace was intentional; there were never protocol kisses, like good morning – peck, see you later – peck. It was the way he looked into my eyes with blazing heat before *every* single kiss. The moments of resistance between our mouths meeting, then being pulled in close. The way he touched me before setting me on fire with his lips. The actual skill of the passionate kiss itself. He always kissed me like he was never going to see me again, even though he was just walking into the kitchen for some water.

At work, we would sneak into other secluded areas and just make out like junior high schoolers, even though we both absolutely knew it was wrong. I couldn't resist being held up against the wall in the racquetball courts with his wandering hands and body pressed against mine. It never went any further than that, though. I guess Cole was lonely in his relationship and I just didn't have one, so I was lonely too. We were simply scratching that companionship itch that we were both craving.

She eventually found out – I believe he told her because she was being such a trash ass girlfriend that it all just came out. And naturally, she jumped into my Facebook inbox, calling me a fat bitch and everything else. But guess what? Had she been spending time with her man, he wouldn't have been able to spend it with me. I don't believe I was his first choice in terms of who to spend time with since he chose to commit to her. But because she was neglectful, it left his time open for someone else. And she can call me fat all she wants, but guess what else? Her man was content with this thickness. And had I been a truly unscrupulous bitch, I absolutely would have fucked him and sent him back to her clown-lookin' ass with all that damn makeup. That's not my style, though. I want to be with someone who only has eyes for me.

But that was like fifteen years ago. Very little like that has happened since, and I don't even typically date men who are separated, because they're still married.

Someone should probably tell that to the new neighbor who was talking to me all recklessly and behaving like I want her husband or something. Ma'am, I don't want your husband – I don't even remember his first name. I want my *own* husband! What I want is for *your* man to find *me* a man. How's he supposed to be *my* soulmate if he's already *yours*? So you can trust that it won't be *me* trying to take him because I don't care to share, like at all. Yet all *they* want to do is share!

If these men would devote even a fraction of the amount of time to date me as they do only trying to *sleep* with me, we could have been married and having sex *against* the white picket fence while the dog watches. But instead, they want to go dippin' and stickin' in every hole in Pittsburgh and then come back to me talking about, "I'm ready to settle down now. You're a good woman, so we should just date now." Talkin' 'bout, "I got the magic stick." No, you got the dumpster dick. And I don't want any of it. You should have just dated me when you had the chance.

♀ ♂ ♀ ♂

Finally, one gentleman who Diana swiped right on seems promising. He's bi-racial – half Greek, half Black, thus quite pleasing to the eye. He's also a musician, so that's another fun thing to have in common. He invited me over to watch a movie. I know what you're thinking. Nope, I made it quite clear that this is not a Netflix and Chill type situation. I plan to be socially distanced with my *own* bag of unshared popcorn.

When I arrive at his townhome, it's cute with nice curb appeal. Vasili invites me into the house, which seems clean and has a number of candles scenting the air. I hope this dude realizes I am dead ass serious about staying as far away from him as possible, because this dimly lit room strongly suggests otherwise.

Vasili is quite the looker, with well-maintained dreadlocks hanging down his back and gray eyes that complement his smooth bronze skin. He's dressed in casual attire, barefoot, with a simple button-down white shirt and khakis.

He hands me a bottled water and we take a seat, he on the loveseat, I on the couch, and proceed to get to know one another in-person. While attempting to make a decision on what movie to watch, I'm startled when two people come down the stairs behind me. *WTF? Who are these people?* They're dressed even more casually than we are.

"Vasss! Didn't know you were having company over! Hi, I'm Sarah." A Caucasian woman wearing boxers and a tee with her hair in a cute, messy ponytail extends her hand to me. I smile and offer her an elbow because... covid. She and her male counterpart venture into the kitchen.

"Ummm, who are they?"

"Oh." Vasili laughs. "That's my nephew and his new wife."

"Ok, but why are they *here* tonight? Because ya know... covid?"

"Nah, it's all good. They get tested daily at work," he states nonchalantly. "Plus, this is their house. I just crash here since my divorce."

Say what now?

"Yeah," he continues. "They asked me to stay with them. They want me here."

"Do they though? You said they're newlyweds," I whisper. "Plus, don't you want your own space? You're fifty years old." I tried to say that in the least judgmental way possible, but it likely didn't come out that way. My bad.

"Nahhh, they like having me here and I like being here, so it's all good. Plus, I have a great bedroom. Lemme show you!"

Wait, what? Is he serious? Last time I visited my sister, my toddler niece wanted to show me her cool new Minnie Mouse room. That is normal. This is not. Full of excitement, Vasili can't wait to drag me upstairs to show me his sleeping quarters.

Now maybe it's for some people, but definitely not for me. Legos. Everywhere. This middle-age man has a bedroom filled with structures created with these decorative blocks, in addition to action figurines. Plastered on all four walls are action/sci-fi movie posters. And the Marvel bedspread on the twin-size bed just tops everything off. I can't help but wonder if he has the matching super hero sheets, but I'm not even going to ask.

"What'ya think? Cool, huh?"

I don't need to actually respond because it *has* to be written all over my face since she doesn't know how to act. See, on my bedroom walls, one will find a mounted fireplace with Bluetooth connectivity to play my sex soundtrack (if I ever get any again). Also visible is a mounted flat-screen tv, sconces, canvas art, you know, *adult shit*. The red Himalayan salt lamps create a sultry red-light district feel at night. *Sexy shit*. I've heard horrible things about stepping on Legos, so I can't bring myself to spend the night and accidentally step on one because I'll fight everyone in this damn house. Outside of the Lego issue, the child-like living situation by a man who will soon receive a senior discount is not exactly a turn on for me. Especially since he reiterated that he didn't plan to seek out his own living space any time soon.

"Don't worry, they won't be able to hear us too much when we're intimate."

Oh, that's perfect since I have no intention of being physically intimate with you in your twin bed – especially in this room that looks like it belongs to one of Alexis' seven kids.

We head back downstairs and get situated in our previously selected seats and resume the movie search.

"Ohh, yeah that one is good," says the man who I've never actually met but has a full mouth of food. The newlyweds re-enter the family area and take seats beside me on the couch, fully intending to join us for this movie date. *So much for the social distancing I requested. There is no way I'm getting through this pandemic without a whole lot of covid.* "Want somma this chicken?" he asks, still chewing, holding his packed plate out in front of me like I would ever take food from a stranger's plate, even *before* there was a highly contagious virus.

I am already super uncomfortable in this situation, but once he starts coughing, that's my cue to exit. Was it tha 'Rona? Probably not. Was he undoubtedly just choking on all that chicken he was shoveling into his mouth? Likely. But I wasn't interested in Vasili or this movie enough to find out. Thank you and good night.

When I arrive home, hanging on my door is a gift bag. I feel like most of my friends have enough common sense to know to hide the bag and not leave it in plain sight of the many people who pass by the house. So because I'm an entire paranoid mess, before even touching the bag, I open my Ring doorbell app to see who left the gift. This trash ass doorbell did not pick up anything, even though somebody was clearly on the porch directly in front of the camera. I'm convinced someone could walk up onto my porch, steal all the furniture, and it *still* would not be picked up by this damn video doorbell. *I need to call them.*

Add to my TO-DO list: Figure out why this damn doorbell can detect the Spirits of the Damned but not actual *living* people

CHAPTER 11

pet peeves

"So will I see you again?" Greg asks on his way out of my house.

"Maybe..." *but probably not.*

He is such a nice, jovial guy, so this is going to sound crazy. I'm well aware of this – I don't need you confirming it. Every person has that *one* weird thing that they cannot tolerate in a person – not just in a significant other, but any human alive in their presence. You stare at that person with widened eyes, like what the actual hell is goin' *on*!?

We had seen each other a few times prior to him visiting my home. This time, the plan was for me to slaughter him in bowling right quick, then grab some wings and pizza to-go afterward. The bowling alley made zero effort to socially distance the lanes by placing a family of six right beside us – yes, even though there were clearly other lanes available. Neither of us felt comfortable in this mask-less environment, so we only bowled the one game and left. Of course I won, so he had to spring for the food.

We took the order back to my house and set up shop in the dining room where we were able to sit appropriately distanced at the six-foot table. He got up to grab paper towels, so I asked that he please bring me one as well. He handed me *one* half-sized sheet and took the giant handful with him to his end of the table. *Um, pardon me sir, why the hell do you find it necessary to use my whole roll of paper towels when we're not even eating saucy foods?*

As we began to chow down on the flavorful cuisine, I paused. I stopped all motion – stopped chewing, breathing, everything. I needed to focus on what that horrific noise was. It was as though someone dropped a herd of cattle in my dining room and they all decided to loudly and recklessly graze simultaneously. Mouth noises when eating foods that shouldn't make noise are especially repulsive to me. Popcorn and chips? Cool. But if I can hear you eating mashed potatoes, I gotta go! I tried my hardest not to stare at this man as he loudly open-mouth chewed every bit of food in front of him. The entire time, all I could think was, *is this how he's teaching his kids to eat?* Again I caught myself staring at the masticated poultry combined with the partially dissolved cheesy dough in his mouth with every chew. *This is going to make me ill.*

He caught me staring. "You ok?" he asked, mouth still full of food.

"Oh uh, yeah... gonna just turn on the music station right quick. Get some sound in here."

As I passed him to get to the television in the living room, I noticed that in just the few minutes we'd been eating, over half of those paper towels had been used. After every *single* bite of food, he had been wiping his mouth to the point of overuse of each paper towel.

With throwback jams now playing, I was certain I would be able to enjoy my food without the sound of his mouth wrecking my appetite, right? Wrong. The loud chomping, chewing, crunching, gnawing, sucking, and smacking audibly persisted to the point my appetite flew south for the winter. I love going out to eat – fine dining in particular. This wretched overabundance of mouth noise cannot happen in an establishment where we're paying over $200 for dinner. I was perturbed that it was happening in my dining room and we only paid $26, with no witnesses.

So I was finished after just two wings and a few bites of pizza. Across the table from me, Greg had loudly consumed all twelve of his wings and two slices of pizza, plus left almost a dozen well-used paper towels all over his end of the table. There was a placemat under there, but it was no longer visible.

Super nice and very handsome guy, but mouth noises turn me all the way off, as does using all of my paper products in one day in the midst of a pandemic-related shortage.

So on his way out, after my ambiguous reply as to whether he'd see me again, Greg calls attention to the gift that's on my door handle still. He jests that he must not be the only one courting me, which I find hilarious because *no one* is actually *courting* me. It's been outside for about four days and no one has called or texted to see if I've gotten it. Ironically, no one has stolen it either.

The next morning, I put on a pair of vinyl gloves, spray the bag down with Lysol, and bring it into the house. Inside, there is an unsigned card, a small day planner, and a bar of Dial soap. I'm not sure what this person is trying to tell me or if I should be offended. Just then, I look up and see the ancient Chinese man smiling really big at my door, with very few teeth still available for use. *It is way too early for this shit.* I subtly slide the screen door window down enough that there's still a barrier between us, but I can make out what he's saying through the thick accent.

"You have a gift now. Birthday," he says with a giant smile.

It's not my birthday.

"Oh, this is from you? Thank you so much."

"Special soap. From China."

I'm pretty sure this came from the Dollar General up the street, but I thank him for his thoughtfulness and generosity anyway. I'm still not sure what made this man think it was my birthday. And because I made the mistake of posting this on social media, all of my friends now have jokes about how I wanted a thoughtful man, so now I have one. I can't help but wonder if he thinks the same thing, considering he just keeps randomly popping up at my house for visits.

♀ ♂ ♀ ♂

In the middle of my workday, my phone rings, and it is none other than Kelvin. I haven't heard from him since I'd declined his offer to cry together on my porch about our problems over cookies and brownies. I inhale deeply and answer my phone, hoping that this man has found someone to help resolve some of his issues, and that he is now in a better place, mentally and emotionally. We begin to catch up and chit chat about work and family and whatnot and then, without even having to ask, I quickly learn that he is not in that better place. Again, I am asked if I will give him an answer to a few questions, seemingly as though he forgot how the last time ended. He wants truthful answers; he knows I am direct and will answer any question asked in the most honest fashion possible – that is, if he actually gets around to it this time.

Again, this man begins to talk... and talk... for *nine* solid minutes this time. I quietly listen as it takes him that excessive length of time to basically say when he was with his wife and they were doing things that should be romantic, it felt like they were just friends and her interest in physical intimacy was not on the same level as his. I did it in seven seconds – it didn't take me anywhere near nine minutes. But he needs to go down the street and around the corner when he talks.

"Pardon me, if I may, I need to stop you for a second." *I'm trying to be as gentle as possible here.* I continue, "It doesn't sound like this topic is something I will be able to answer questions about. You really need to see if your wife will have a candid sit down with you and answer any questions you have about the relationship and intimacy, or lack thereof."

"Well, I did that already, and that's why I feel bad."

"Oh, you did? Ok, well then that's good!" I reply excitedly. "What was her response?"

Silence... Still silence, then a long sigh.

"See! This is why I can't talk to you! This is why I stopped talking to you in the first place!"

What the actual fuck just happened here?

"You won't let me talk!" he yells.

Is this nut roll for real? I literally sat here in total silence and let him ramble on for nine solid minutes. Have you ever listened to someone talk straight through for that length of time about total randomness? I have a day job with real shit to do!

"I just want to tell my story and you won't let me!"

Jesus, take the wheel! Bite your tongue, Renée. Don't say anything. Just shut up. Nope, can't even do it. ACTUAL insensitivity coming in 3... 2... "Then you need to call Oprah. I sat quietly and listened to you for almost ten minutes – said not a single word, letting you tell your story, but at some point you *gotta* get to the damn point and ask whatever question it is that you need to ask. There's not enough money in the federal reserve to convince me that communication was not an issue in every single relationship you've ever had, because this level of response is not normal."

A good therapist would be more than happy to listen for a whole sixty minutes and bill his talkative, disjointed, non-getting to the point ass accordingly. And if he just needs an ear, then he should stop prefacing each talk with, "Can I ask you something?" Ok, n*ow* I probably won't hear from him again, and I'm completely ok with that.

Add to my TO-DO list: Buy some chlorine because clearly someone has peed and left some covid in this shallow ass dating pool

CHAPTER 12

just give me some sperm... please

Oh, my damn! How is my street not the location for some insane reality TV show? It's like every time I'm outside or even looking out the large window in my living room, I see the craziest shit ever. Look, if you need to steal a shopping cart *from* the store, put your kids *in* it to take them back down *to* the store (from which you stole the cart) to grocery shop *and* it appears as though you have another child on the way!? I'mma need for you to get your ass on the pill until you can get it together. Because I've seen it *all*!

Scratch that. Watching the *extra* hood folks in the domestic disturbance apartments next door chainsaw an entire *car* in half on my way out to go to work? *Now* I've seen it all. What *for*!? At this point, I'm half tempted to call in sick on the one day I *do* work in person now, so I can see what these fools do with half a car! I feel like this is way more important than my actual job.

♀ ♂ ♀ ♂

This *must* be "Stalker Week" for Renée! I have eight missed calls from Ohio on my *office* phone with no messages left. No one should be calling me from another state in this current position. Finally, Dani transfers a call to me. Turns out it's a dude I used to talk to *years* ago! He found where I work on LinkedIn and has been calling incessantly ever since. Nice guy but had a vasectomy at age twenty-four after having only *one* child. Um, y'all know my eggs are *dying* to be penetrated like ASAP so that didn't work for me!

"Hey! It's Bruno. Do you remember me?"

"Yes, did you have your vasectomy reversed?"

"That's the *first* question you ask me? Not how are you?" He laughs. "No, I didn't."

"Oh, ok. So what made you decide to call then?"

This man knew back then I wanted nothing more than to eventually become a mother. That hasn't changed, so if you can neither impregnate me, nor afford to help me impregnate my*self*, we literally have nothing to discuss.

Dani adjusts her mask as she stands to look over the glass to my cube. "Sooo who was Bruno with the southern accent?"

"Nosey much?"

"Damn right," she exclaims in a volume that leads Everett to remove his other earbud to see what's going on. He pulls up his mask, comes over, and they both stand staring at me expectantly.

For the life of me, I can't figure out why we're even back in the office right now. Granted, it's only one to two days per week, but for my germophobic ass, that's two days too many, considering we don't *need* to be here to get this work done.

"Ok, well you can't just say 'vasectomy' all loud in the workplace and not expect us to come investigate," Everett states.

There's literally nothing to tell here. "What I would like to know is who the hell has been eating at my desk?"

"What?" questions Everett. "Why would any of us eat at *your* desk?"

"Well there are chocolate sprinkles everywhere on this side desk. I haven't been here and I haven't had any donuts."

I start sliding my hand across the desk to gather what appeared to be easily forty or so sprinkles into a pile to discard when Dani runs over frantically with a bottle of sanitizer yelling, "Noooo! Those aren't sprinkles! Stoppp!"

She immediately begins spraying me while I start screaming back, "What the hell is it!?"

"MOUSE POOP!" she cries.

Then I scream even more because I *touched* it with my *bare* hands!

Everett just stands by shaking his head watching in amusement as we jump and shriek until I accidentally get spritzed in the mouth with sanitizer. I go to wash my trembling hands with actual soap and scalding hot water, then disinfect my tainted work station – twice. *Swear if anyone takes me to HR for sanitizing my work station now, I will fight everyone in this building!* Especially after I had opened the overhead bin and even *more* mouse poop rained down onto my desk. Those greedy little bastards had devoured an entire pack of eight caramel rice cakes and half a pack of hot chocolate mix!

I begin packing up my stuff because a family of mice used my desk as a toilet, and I'm not staying in this cramped room with people breathing pandemic air.

"It's only noon. Where are you going?" Dani asks.

"Home," I say flatly.

"You're not completing the day?"

"No."

"Did you ask Kathy?"

"No."

"Well, do you think you should?"

"No, what's she gonna say? No?"

"Yes!" they both exclaim.

"No. She can't *make* me stay somewhere I'm not comfortable. So I can either finish my day from home or take personal time. But either way, I'm leaving."

I explain to them that in therapy, we've been discussing boundaries and how I am consistently doing things or going places I don't want to because someone *else* wants me to. And that literally includes work. If this pandemic has shown us nothing else, it's that life is too short to continuously be placed in shitty situations where I don't care to be, or doing things for people I don't want to do. So, no means no, people! Stop asking.

No, I will not lend you $250 that I will never see again.

No, I will not be your personal taxi for your $2 in "gas money" *WTF?*

No, I don't want to sell your hair, beauty, diet, or jewelry products.

No, I will not date you if your man breasts are bigger than my gargantuan lady breasts.

And no, I will not show them to you or send pics.

No, I will not sleep with you if you have a woman.

No, you cannot smoke in my car or my house. *Really?*

No, you cannot bring your five kids under eight years old to my home.

And *hell* no, I won't babysit your three badass kids that *you* can't even control.

I have no problem saying no, so you should probably ask for normal shit.

"So does that mean you'll finally stop giving me those *un*requested sexy time dances now? Please?" Dani asks, hopefully.

"No. Absolutely not."

When I pull up my mask and start to sing Tina Turner's hit song Private Dancer while doing my best thick-girl pole moves in front of Dani's cube, that's poor Everett's signal to refill his coffee again. Plus, with the limited knowledge he has of me, I feel like he knows that if I try to drop it like it's hot, he'll have to help pick me back up.

♀ ♂ ♀ ♂

It is early as hell Saturday morning. My phone has been vibrating and I'm so hesitant to check it because it's always some crazy shit nowadays. And look at that, I'm not even wrong. One is a text that came in late last night from an unsaved number that I don't recognize:

Hey. I know we haven't talked in a few years. I thought about your moms the other day and wondered how she was doin with her tall sexy self.

I could feel myself retch as I deleted that message. First of all, who are you and why are you randomly thinking about my senior citizen mother? That's just tremendously creepy. If she would stop answering my phone like she's about to lick whoever is on the other end of it, I wouldn't have these problems with men. This isn't the phone sex hotline. And it wouldn't be the first time men have called for me but wanted to stay on the phone with *her* if she answered.

The others were new messages from the dating app, the first from a man with a screen name from which no good can possibly come.

SayMyName69: I'll be your milk kind sweetheart I'm hung I'll milk that P so good

Of course, I was right. Delete.

Not *every* man I interact with is completely insane on these apps. Some initiate a normal message but lack the ability to keep the most basic conversation going. It's really not rocket science. Questions generate conversation, simple statements do not. So ask a damn question. I will answer it, say something witty, then ask one back. This cycle repeats until there is smooth conversation that doesn't even require a question anymore. But I meet men to whom I'm asking all the questions and they're just answering them. Hey dork, I work in advertising, not criminal justice. I did not swipe right only to have to interrogate you because you're not capable of a normal back-and-forth interaction. So, delete. It gets exhausting having to constantly do all the conversation maintenance. Then there are those conversations where they have allll the words to say, but none of them make any damn sense!

I mean, maybe I'm just getting stupider as the year wears on, because... covid. *Yes, I absolutely plan to blame covid for everything that is wrong with me.* I asked this man what he did for a living, and I still don't understand any of what he just said. And I don't think I could actually pinpoint what his occupation is, so I had to reach out to my friends on social media for help. They are unable to assist and feel just as confused as I do.

Holy Roller 18: My thing in life now is to empower are people always try to use lack of knowledge and lack of resources to justify their inequities so I partner up with the church and a lot of stuff I do to myself to help people read answers to society and also the youth startup businesses and I and I'm linking with these churches to do fundraising so now we can talk we must support our own.

If you figure it out, message me. Like, for real, because I seriously just need basic answers like, manager, engineer, etc...

Me: I'm not sure if it's because you didn't punctuate and it's all kinda running together or what, but none of it made any sense to me and I still can't actually tell what you do for a living

Holy Roller 18: Just call me.

Not a chance in hell. I am legit running out of patience here... and time. Plus, he never left a number.

I pull up to the doctor's office for my 8am appointment. I'm a few minutes early, so I just sit in the parking lot, truly contemplating why I'm about to put myself through yet *another* procedure in an effort to get pregnant. I am old, well I *feel* old anyway. And I'm drained – emotionally from all the failed and/or unsuccessful conception attempts, and physically because these hormones wreak havoc on my body. I'm moody, cranky, bloated, short-tempered and hangry all the damn time – what's worse, it's at the *same* time! Don't even get me started on all the headaches from my hormones constantly being in flux on a daily basis. Oh, now shall we discuss the $74,000 I have spent so far? Please realize I could've purchased an entire pregnant *person* for that amount. Or more reasonably, I could've adopted at least four children by now. But the doctors for years had been telling me, "Everything in there is fine; your bloodwork is normal; eventually one will stick because your uterine lining is *gorrrgeous*!" What an odd compliment. *Thank you*? But alas, nearly six figures later, I still only have a moody cat.

When I exit my car to finally enter the building, a *very* elderly lady in the next car calls out to me, "If you see Susan in there, tell her to hurry up and bring her ass out here!"

I pause mid-step, certain she must be addressing someone else, "I'm sorry, I don't know Susan, Ma'am."

"Oh, you'll know her when you see her," she says resolutely.

Ok lady... I swear the weirdest stuff happens to me! I just want to have one normal day.

Because the front doors are locked on weekends, Saturday appointments enter directly into the fertility office through the back door that happens to be propped open with a large rock. As I enter the building, a chipmunk scurries in ahead of me and takes off racing down the hall! *OMG this is not ok! If that thing gets locked in there and dies, that foul stench of decomp will ruin some poor woman's day.* Can you even imagine some unsuspecting patient positioning her legs wide open into the stirrups and an atrocious odor of death wafts up from beneath her in the speculum drawer? *I better tell someone.*

Like in a distorted version of Alice in Wonderland, I follow the rodent down the hall toward the main doctor's office where I'm *not* supposed to be, when a bossy-looking nurse comes out of an office.

Before she can reprimand me, I inform her, "Umm, excuse me, there's a chipmunk in here."

She looks at me suspiciously and says, "Nooo." Like it's totally out of the realm of possibilities when you have the door propped open to a whole ass forest on the other side of your narrow parking lot.

"Yessss, I saw him come in. He went in that office on the right."

Finally realizing I was serious, because who for real makes that shit up this early in the morning, the nurse closes the door and writes on the white-board that's affixed, "DO NOT ENTER CHIPMUNK INSIDE!" Ok, well that just sounds like a colossal joke in itself.

"So, what are you gonna do?"

"I dunno, we gotta get it out though," she says urgently, looking around for a few reinforcements to assist.

I'm over here thinking we need to set a trap. So from the adjacent office, I grab a rectangular plastic garbage can and a sheet. I share my plan to place this trashcan in the doorway so it can't escape into the rest of the office, but we need someone to go in and coax or scare it out.

I tell the nurse, "I need you to hold this sheet, and when he scurries into this garbage can trap, I'll pick it up quickly and you just throw the sheet over top of it and we're good."

"Yeah, yeah, I can do that. Just throw the sheet on top of the can," she stammers, nodding frantically and turning paler by the second. That shit's not sounding so believable. She is sweating and shaking when she not so calmly informs me that she's petrified of vermin.

Another nurse goes into the office to hunt for the little fuzzball, "I don't see it... I don't see it," then lets out a high-pitched squeal and jumps up onto the doctor's desk once she finally *does* see it. "There's really a chipmunk in here!" *No shit. But how is you being up on that desk helpful right now?*

"I need you to lure the thing to us so it runs into this trash can," I call out to her.

She slowly comes down from the desk, and with a lot of nervous prancing and grunting from the nurse, the chipmunk finally makes a mad dash toward us. I have my hands on the trash can ready to do my part of this – ya know, that part I absolutely didn't sign up for – but at the last second, the nurse who's holding the sheet freaks out, yelps, throws the sheet at my *face,* then runs down the hall screaming. Amidst the hysterics, she disrupts the trap and the furry fugitive escapes. While she's sprinting down the hall screaming, the chipmunk is chasing *her*, and there are *five* of us now chasing the chipmunk down this damn hall.

We manage to corner it but it eludes us again and scampers into the blood draw lab, so we shut the door and again, still winded, I reiterate the battle plan.

I grab *another* garbage can and sheet. "Alright look, same trap, different people." Because my trap was effective, *that* bitch, however, was not.

As we're preparing to tackle this situation *again*, something happens that feels like a slow motion scene from a suspense movie. A large door suddenly swings open from behind us and this chick bursts through it like she's been waiting her whole life for this moment! I don't even know where she came from, but she slaps on a pair of latex gloves and stomps over like a boss bitch! She 'bout to go in there and catch Alvin with her bare hands! For a brief moment, I wonder to myself if *this* gladiator is the Susan the old lady in the parking lot asked me to relay the message to. If so, I'm not sending her out there until she catches this chipmunk!

Now see, that's some shit my crazier white friends would do because I'm trying to tell you, I was the only Black person in this entire office, and I was *not* about to touch this thing with my bare hands. Look, I will *help,* but this bitch is not about to catch a chipmunk with *any* part of her body. So this gladiator chick goes in like a boss! The nurses and I are staring at each other intently, hearing all this commotion, banging and screeching going on behind the closed door. Items can be heard loudly falling to the ground, followed by a mass of swear words. We are thoroughly convinced that she's in there being *murdered* by this chipmunk. She says the word, so I open the door and set the trap. He scurries in – almost jumps out – but I throw the sheet over the garbage can *myself* this time. Thankfully, I was dressed for the full-speed Olympic sprint I did through the office with the garbage can, frantically shouting, "Open the door! Open the door!"

Upon releasing Alvin to his family, I decide in my mind that if I get a bill for today's visit, all seven shades of hell shall be raised, because I am *not* paying that shit! They owe *me* money. I am here for a fifteen-minute procedure but spend forty minutes helping the three stooges catch a woodland creature and release it so that it didn't starve to death, die and funk up the entire office. So I'm trying to tell you, if they request that $20 co-pay, there's about to be consequences and repercussions!

Add to my TO-DO list: Find an actual human with sperm that doesn't swim in circles to handle this

CHAPTER 13
the connection – or lack thereof

So I decided to try something new last night. And now that I'm up, I should absolutely text my mom about it since it's something she's been bugging me about for ages!

Me: So I finally slept without panties on for the 1st time in YEARS!!

Mama: Well Yay!!! That musta been liberating!!

Me: No. It was weird. I didn't like it.

Mama: It has to BREATHE Renée!! *Siiigh* Oh that POOOOOR thing...

Me: "That pooooor thing?" Lmao are u referring my precious va-gemstone!?

Mama: YEESSSSSSS!!!!!

Mama: Wait, your WHAT?

Seriously never telling her anything again. I like to wear panties – leave me alone. I have about one hundred forty pairs, most of which are Victoria's Secret, so they all need to be worn. The contents of that one drawer are more expensive than some of the furniture I own. I calculated it to make sure it got included in the homeowner's coverage. If anything were to happen to the house, I needed to make sure this drawer could be fully re-stocked with the delicate unmentionables to which I have grown accustomed.

Scrounging through this meticulously organized panty drawer, I locate and don my cute white boy-shorts with the mesh sides and my new black and white Nick Marzock tee. Comfort is a necessity as I thoroughly clean the bathroom and the kitchen while rockin' out to his music, singing into a spatula – in my boy-shorts and T-shirt. At random intervals, I sit around the house and play online – yes, still in my boy shorts and T-shirt. So how I could *forget* I was in said attire when I step outside to get the mail and stand at the edge of the porch with my hands on my hips in a 'superman' stance is totally beyond me! People are driving by staring and smiling. *WTF, why are they staring up here?*

That is, until a beige car pulls up and honks at me. I can see Jenna in the passenger seat gesturing to me with shoulder shrugs and a wide-eyed expression, then shouts out the window, "Wow, aren't we a classy bitch?!"

I look at her, so confused, until a nice warm breeze blows over me and I realize, *oh, that's why all those people were driving by staring.* I'm sucking at life. Even though they have seen my secret garden, I run in embarrassed and throw on some shorts before Jenna and her hubby Marco make it up the walk to my home.

"Are you decent?" she asks before opening my door. "This is not quite the welcome we expected." Jenna laughs as we exchange hugs.

"Yeah, we need to come by here more often!" Marco jokes in a thick Belizean accent.

They make the absolute cutest couple. And I love the way, at the very least, they *look* like they love each other. So the weirdo that I am, about an hour into the visit, I begin to ask them couples questions, Newlywed Game style. The questions start out innocent enough, like, which of you has the worst temper? Who is most likely to apologize first? And they seem to easily agree on all of the questions asked. But of course, I have to throw some spicy ones in there.

"So, who is more sexually adventurous?"

"She is," he answers first.

"I had to *make* him have sex on the beach with me on a vacation," Jenna says in shock.

"OMG! How?"

"Well, in the golf cart." She laughs. "It was really dark and secluded, so we were able to get it done without anyone seeing."

"I am so jealous. Last time I had sex outside was in college in a public park with Jeremy. The police came around the corner with that giant spotlight that's on top of the car, pointed it directly at us and said, 'park's about to close, you need to leave.' Thank heavens he had *just* finished. If he would have lasted any longer than his usual six minutes, we would have absolutely been in jail!"

"And on the sex offender registry," Jenna adds, grinning. "*Children* are in parks! But just six minutes, though?"

Marco looks at us like we're being judgmental and shakes his head. "Maybe he was just nervous?"

"This was not our first time! We had done it before, just not outside. And it always lasted around five-six minutes and he would always blame me, talkin' 'bout 'she's too juicy.' If you consistently can't keep your dick hard longer than six minutes, you don't get to blame that on me. You feel like you're about to blow, pull out. Regroup. Think about politics. Dive back in. This is not rocket science."

"But we men have a lot of pressure on us. The male body is very complicated. All of the blood just goes from our entire brain into that one place."

Even though Marco said that with all the seriousness in the world, Jenna and I burst out laughing because a lot of men are giving that *one place way* too much credit. There's not enough space in some of those men's *one place* to even accommodate the amount of blood that the body wants to send there. But if Marco is packing heat in that department, that might explain his sentiment.

"We have blood flow too, man. And our bodies are way more complicated than yours," Jenna argues. "When we get aroused, our lower region throbs, becomes engorged, and ready for attention too. You guys aren't special." She laughs. "And trying to achieve the female orgasm is like stumbling across a purple spotted unicorn for so many women."

"Girl, right?! I ordered this G-spot wand because I was hell-bent on a mission to find mine. I know she *was* in there! But I'm almost positive that bitch has since packed up and left town!"

They laugh, but I am dead ass serious.

"It's this long pink stick and on the end of it is a vibrating bullet. So feeling adventurous, I was rooting around in there trying to find it... Nothing. So I ended up just finishing the job the tried-and-true way."

"You have never had an orgasm from actual sex?" Jenna asks, surprised. I shake my head no.

"Ohhh my Gosh," Marco whines in his adorable accent. "What are the men here *doing*? I'm so sorry for my entire male gender for depriving you of the pleasure that you should be getting on a very regular basis. You need to come home with us and get taken care of."

Silence quickly descends upon the room like a menacing black cloud. Jenna frowns and looks over at him. My eyes widen and I look at both of them like, what kind of freaky shit are y'all actually into that no one told me about?

Finally realizing how that sounded, he bursts out laughing. "Ohhh, no no no. I meant home as in my home country, not my house!" he says, still laughing. "We're not that freaky yet! I heard we're leaving that to you."

"Wait, you heard what now? How can I be that freaky when I'm not even getting any regularly?"

"Wifey said you have some sort of rope contraption on the bed. I kinda wanna see it. Can you bring it down?"

"That's not a thing, babe," Jenna laughs. "It's literally attached, in a sense, to the bed. You would have to go up to check it out."

Without missing a beat, Marco is halfway up the steps on the way to my master bedroom. So we, of course, get up and follow him because he'll probably have questions. He's never been upstairs before, but he's moving like my room is at the end of the yellow brick road and knows that he's supposed to follow it.

Slowly entering my pristine sleeping quarters, they find the bed adorned in gold with six plush decorative pillows as the focal point of the room. He stands staring at the elegant structure, appearing confused because everything in my sleep chamber looks so incredibly classy.

"I was expecting some sort of sex dungeon type bedroom with red or black walls. This is really nice. Where is the rope contraption?"

Jenna giggles as I saunter over to the foot of the bed and pull one of the thick well-hidden restraints from between the base and the mattress and dramatically drape it on to the striking gold bedspread.

Marco's eyes widen. "I thought y'all were playin'!"

"Renée don't play about restraints, mi amor," Jenna says confidently as she exits the room.

"So do you have a swing too?" he asks curiously, following her out.

"Babe!" She playfully hits him with the back of her hand and shoots him that 'stop being nosey' look.

Sadness overcomes me because unfortunately, I do not. But knowing my sister, one might just arrive in the mail one day.

We continue our naughty sex chat downstairs, where I work diligently to convince him that every couple should have a four-point restraint system on the bed.

♀ ♂ ♀ ♂

On the porch (in pants this time), I say to my dietician on our video chat, "Ok, but it doesn't really count if you put it in your mouth right quick but spit it out."

Blank stare from the lady walking her dog past my house. Little does she know that I was simply referencing the calories in the moon pie I just tasted for the first time and didn't like, so I spit it out. Maybe I should just take my virtual appointments *inside* from now on.

I am seriously having the *weirdest* day! I should've just gone in the house after that appointment ended, but nooooo, stupid here wants to just enjoy the fresh air. And here comes the ancient Chinese man smiling enthusiastically and informing me that he is here to tell me my future. I let him know I don't really need my future told to me, but he insists repeatedly and tells me to give him a pen. He asks for my name, my birthday, and then my signature. So naturally, my first thought is this old ass man is about to try to steal my identity and ruin my stellar credit.

I give him my name along with the month and day of my birthday, but no signature. He takes the pen, gets ridiculously comfortable on my porch, and starts doing all of this mathematical work and excitedly informs me I will have a spouse this year. Two, in fact! Not sure of the laws overseas, but sir, that's not legal in this state. He goes on to inform me that one will be a good guy and the other will be a bad guy, so I have to basically choose the right one. Well, now I *know* he must have missed some medication because I can barely find a functional *boyfriend*, let alone an entire spouse. But I'm just going to see what the rest of the year holds and see if he is correct.

As he moseys off my porch pleased with his predictions regarding my love life, my phone jingles and I feel a lump in the pit of my stomach. I can't help but to feel a little anxious when I see I have matches because so far, none of them have been solid. But here goes nothin'. There are two who matched and left messages.

Main14U: Hello beautiful, you up for dinner a movie a lot of pleasure then a game of chess?

Abso-freakin-lutely not. Delete.

The other, I decide to message purely for superficial reasons. He's handsome but doesn't have anything written in his profile.

Mr. Slimm: Hey. How are you?

Me: Too tired lol. How are you?

Mr. Slimm: 6' 1" You?

Me: ??? Is that you offering me your height when asked how you were? LOL

Mr. Slimm: Sorry 41.

And that's what I get for being shallow. I rest my head in my hands and just exhale. Nope. I'm tappin' out of this conversation. If you can't follow along with the most basic exchange, I can't bring you to the company holiday party either. It's sad that that's become the standard for whether or not I can date someone.

After enjoying the modern-day soap opera that is my street, where yet *another* man just opened the car door to vomit at the stop sign in front of my house, finished, closed the door and drove off, it's time for me to take my ass back in the house. Like, why do these people think my street doubles as a toilet!? I'm not sure if he just thought he wouldn't be seen because it's dark or what, but I'm done with this entire town today.

I begin to straighten up the mess I made on the porch and no sooner than I switch off the fire, a motorcycle stalls at the stop sign in front of my house. Yup, right beside the vomit.

My trash ass paternal unit is a biker and rides one similar to this person's. He put me on the back of his motorcycle at four years old and I've been hooked ever since. So I can't help but to be severely attracted to a man on two wheels – I love to ride, and I'm an excellent passenger. In fact, the only life lessons he ever instilled in me were, "If you gon to get on the back of someone's bike, make sure they always have a helmet for you. If you don't have no helmet, you don't ride." And then he handed me the sturdiest leather bike jacket that one could ever imagine and said, "Always wear jeans and *this*. It's hot in the summer, but don't ever ride with your legs exposed." And with that, at fourteen years of age, I think he felt his parenting was complete. I never understood that last one until I saw a motorcycle accident and half of someone's thigh was torn apart.

I notice he is struggling to get the bike started, so I stay on the porch just in case he might need some help, since it's 11:30 at night. He manages to push the bike out of the intersection and begins to investigate the problem while looking around to assess his surroundings.

I peer over the ledge and shout, "Hey, are you ok?"

"I think my battery is dead."

Not sure why I keep engaging with random strangers lately, but I'm positive that I will one day be held captive in my own basement. It wouldn't be a far stretch, because it goes *down* on my street. Some of the most horrible things in life have happened on this street in the past year of me owning this house. That's probably why the Spirits of the Damned feel so comfortable here. Four doors down, the neighbor murdered her two children.

Two doors down from that, the man murdered his wife. And I want to say in between those two houses, a man killed him*self*. So I probably need to hasten that whole license-to-carry situation. Still, I walk over to this tall, helmeted, leather-clad stranger anyway. He removes his helmet and OMG there is a very handsome chocolate man under there. I had no idea if it was even a man or a woman, Black or white; I was just intent on helping a biker in need. This is definitely a bonus.

"I'm about an hour or so from home and I'm not really that familiar with this area, so thank you so much for asking. Do you, by chance, have jumper cables?"

I lease a new Hyundai every three years, so what use would I have for jumper cables? But my mother, the eternal safety patrol, made sure I have every possible safety item I could ever need in my vehicle. There's a standing light, an entire car tool kit, pop-up safety cones, and of course, jumper cables. I can't even think of all the rest, but I'm positive I could perform minor surgery with the first aid kit that's in the back seat. "I do, actually. I don't know how old they are, but we can try it."

He pushes his bike over to my driveway while I make a quick call to my mom to let her know that a strange biker is outside of my house, in case I go missing. Then I grab the cables and pop the hood for him to do what he does. I absolutely should have been paying attention, because while my paternal unit was giving me advice on how to ride a motorcycle, he never taught me the normal things that every woman should actually know, like how to jump a dead battery.

This very handsome man tells me that his biker name is Gemini. He tells me his real name, but I am kind of entranced by his smooth mocha skin and beautiful smile under the amber streetlights, so I miss it. He also continues to thank me profusely for my assistance. I don't quite understand why he is so grateful until he explains how, at that corner, he looked around and saw nothing but political signage. In this day and age, he didn't necessarily feel comfortable just walking up to a random house as a Black man covered in leather and knocking. As a Black woman, I completely understand his plight.

We continue to chat while the battery charges, in hopes that it will actually work. Then he continues on his way to his destination because it's absolutely going to rain. No phone numbers are exchanged during our encounter, so maybe he is already committed. But it was still nice to have some functional interaction with a seemingly normal man. Maybe there's hope for me yet.

Add to my TO-DO list: Stash lock picks in random places of my basement just in case

CHAPTER 14
buyer beware

This stupid pandemic is ruining my birthday, though I *did* receive a delivery of the most gorgeous yellow roses and white calla lilies. Initially thinking they're from my mom, since all nice things usually are, I promptly video call her to yell at her for spending money that she doesn't have. There are a dozen and a half flowers here; these could *not* have been cheap. She's looking at me so confused and then I realize they're from the Rapunzel guy. Even though he has a girlfriend, this is the sweetest gesture ever. Those are my two favorite flowers and no man has ever paid attention to me even mentioning it, let alone taken action. *Now I just need a single man to try this.* I reach out to him to offer my most sincere thank you, as it truly meant a lot and brightened my day. *But no, you still can't smash if you have a girlfriend... or if you're not trying to actually date me.*

What's normally a large group on hand to celebrate indoors has been reduced to six for a socially distanced outdoor gathering. Liza suggested

Top Golf since I'd never been before. I was supposed to be in Las Vegas celebrating, but we'll just have to be weird and wild here. Pro golfers Liza, Alexis, and Dani join us amateurs, me, Jenna, and Brie.

As is standard practice, Alexis is my designated driver, even though I don't *plan* to drink like I did at the last birthday party. And of course, as the sky is blue, Dani shows up late. She rushes in and hugs me anyway despite her covid concerns. "Happy birthday! Did I miss the update?" she asks, breathing heavily, waving to each of the group members.

She hands me a gift bag.

"What update?" I ask.

"Your sexy specialisssst," she replies.

"Yess, please do update us on your mighty mentorrrr," Alexis says in a sultry voice.

"I prefer the title, life coach cutieee," Jenna adds.

Meanwhile, Liza is shaking her head, starting to blush, as usual.

"All these names for a man none of you have ever seen?"

Brie chimes in, "Bitch, you know damn well we looked him up!"

Of course they did. What was I thinking?

"Well, I wanna see him!" Dani whines while Alexis pulls him up on her phone.

"Ohhhhh... yeahhh... ok." Dani nods in approval.

She passes her phone to Jenna, who shows Liza because we all know she is *definitely* not looking up strange men on her phone. She's my *normal* friend.

"Woww... he's pretty handsome. Maybe I *do* need a little more therapy in my life." She winks and everyone laughs because my sweet Liza can be pretty saucy when she wants to be.

I run to the bathroom because I'm not even gonna dignify any of that with a response. As I leave, I can still hear them creating sexy nicknames for him, snickering like schoolgirls.

"What's wrong?" Liza questions when she notices me jogging back toward the table.

"Ohh emmm geeee!" I turn to look behind me. "Thank God for these masks, like for real! I bumped into the dude with the five kids who wanted to split the $33 food bill at The Improv last year after I had already paid for *everything* else! Like, physically we ran *into* each other while I was exiting the bathroom! I would know his green eyes anywhere. I apologized, as did he, and I don't think he recognized me!"

"You have pretty distinct features, even behind a mask. How could he not?" asks Liza.

Alexis interjects, "Maybe he did, but was just embarrassed, so he played it off?"

"Either way, I'm fine with it," I laugh. "Come on y'all, I got the text that our area is ready."

As we're walking past the other golf bays, unbeknownst to me, Brie taps Jenna and points out an exquisite manly specimen. Last time these bitches were together in the mall and they "found me a man," it turned out to be the "pizza and parolee" guy! I'm gonna have to start separating them when we're out. But either way, despite the ring on her finger, Brie can detect a hottie from 1,000 paces.

When we make it to our bay, I turn to see Jenna and Brie bringing up the rear, finally making it over. Then behind them, a tall, caramel, neatly constructed man follows. When he approaches, he says that my friends told him it was my special day, so he felt obliged to pay me a birthday wish. His smooth skin and seemingly well-crafted facial hair were obscured by his mask, but he had amazing hazel eyes and a deep voice. He leaves me with his card, and we all stare at his perfectly sculpted hind quarters as he walks back to his group three bays down. *Ok, maybe they did a better job this time.*

We're all discussing how nice looking he is while glancing in that direction, and then it happens. He pulls his mask down to laugh and take a drink.

"DAAAAAYMMMM!" they all lean and yell like Craig and Smokey in the movie Friday. I can't see what *they're* seeing because he's too far away. Curse this damn astigmatism that was on my to-do list and never got done!

"That mouth is *HIT*," Brie exclaims with bass in her voice to emphasize just *how* tore up it is.

"Waaait, what's wrong with –"

"That's a *BIG* ol' rusty bucket of nnnnope!" Jenna interrupts as she takes the card from me, rips it up, and tosses it in the trash of the next bay.

Ok, maybe these masks aren't so helpful after all.

So the only problem I'm left with, now that my friends have spared me from that dental disaster, is that the Bosom of Life is so large that it is prohibiting me from being able to hold the club and swing correctly. As a result, these dusty heifers are very much enjoying recording my ineptitude to plaster all over social media. I will most definitely need to see my chiro, Dr. Jake, after this calamity.

♀ ♂ ♀ ♂

I don't have my glasses on for the second day in a row, but I would know that physique and gait anywhere. Though he has crossed my mind often, I haven't seen him in about eight months. Thank heavens I'm wearing my mask because beneath it, I am looking like the seventh circle of hell. It's Walmart. I am not checking for anyone in this store, so while I don't visit the establishment in night-clothes and slippers like some in the photos found online, I definitely don't look like my best self right now. I am in the largest sweats I own with my hair in a bun, literally just here for some salad and ice cream. No judgment, please.

As Diego glides toward me in his gray sweatpants that just beg every woman to gaze at his ample crotch, he gives me a warm smile, of course with no mask on because he never learns.

I'm trying to remain cool as he approaches, considering my anger at the way he ghosted me is bubbling to the surface.

"How you doin'?" he asks with his sly smirk and sexy accent.

I simply smile and nod. All that is visible are my eyes, and I'm certain anyone looking can see the hurt and disappointment behind them because they don't hide emotion well.

"Well, you lookin' good."

This man is literally still lying. "Thank you, so do you, of course."

He shoots me that suggestive but bashful grin that he's known for, because of course he *knows* he looks good as hell. Nothing has changed there.

"So what's new wit'chu? You workin' on your next project?" he asks.

I love how men will talk to you like nothing is wrong, like they did nothing erroneous, like everything is completely ok, when they know damn well it isn't.

"I am," I state awkwardly. "What's new with you?"

"Oh nothin', same ol' same. Jus' workin' out and stuff."

I stand staring into his hazel eyes, waiting to see if he's going to say anything else, but he doesn't. Is this man seriously omitting his engagement right now? Like you put a ring on another woman's finger and are about to scoot her ass down the aisle and you don't have *anything* to say about that when asked "what's new?" *Does he think I don't know?*

Breaking the awkward silence, "Sooo, I heard you're engaged. Didn't wanna mention that? Or that's not new enough?"

He pauses to try to play it off. "Oh yeah, that. Yeah, you know... Ummm..."

More awkward silence.

"So you don't have anything to say about it? About the fact that you just basically ghosted me and popped up engaged again for the *second* time?"

"I didn't ghost you. You was wit' that guy an' I was pissed about it."

Diego has clearly been vaping too much and it *must* be eating through his brain. Have I spoken to other men? Absolutely, because we're both single and he wasn't interested in a commitment. And we see how those conversations have gone, but was I *seeing* people *while* I was seeing him? Absolutely not. The man basically consumed my every thought.

"I was not with any other person while dealing with you, and you know it. You were literally coming to my home *regularly,* completely unannounced. If I were even *trying* to see someone else, I would've absolutely squashed those unannounced visits. Plus, I know how you get."

He's one of those men who is convinced everyone is lying and cheating on him, because *he's* the one doing the *actual* lying and cheating. So he projects his ill behavior onto the other person.

"I seen him. There was a guy who was on your porch leavin' you pop. You wasn't home."

Am I hearing this correctly? He's mad at me and I wasn't even home?

"Do you seriously realize how insane you sound? So you saw a man drop pop off onto my porch when I *wasn't* home and that was enough for you to just disappear from my life?" That could've been a Door Dash delivery for all he knew!

"I didn't like it. Why was he bringin' you pop?"

I literally dodged a fucking bullet here because what kind of insanity is this? What kind of toxic relationship would this be if this man is ready to walk out on me because somebody left a few two-liter bottles of pop on my property – when I wasn't even home?

"Yes, now that I think of it, a man *did* leave pop on my porch – my neighbor, Gabriel, who is over sixty and *gay*. That man wants *no* parts of me. But he *does* know that blackberry Canada Dry is my favorite."

"It wasn't your neighbor; it was a Black guy."

Gabriel is also Puerto Rican and he had been in the sun all summer, which definitely darkened his complexion. He is absolutely not Black, but none of that matters because this is the dumbest shit I have ever heard in my entire life.

"That man could have bought me a bag of dancing dildos and it literally would not matter because you and I were not together. And if it *did* matter that much to you, *if I mattered*, the fact that you're *that* immature that you can't talk to me to find out what's actually going on?" I lower my voice, "Be salty when the man who is bringing me the pop enters my house and you see me drop to my knees to say 'thank you' for the generosity. Hell, I've sucked *your* dick in front of an open door before... and for much less than pop."

We quietly go back and forth like this for a good five more minutes, with him gaslighting me until I finally put an end to it. It's whatever at this point, because I don't need this level of narcissism in my life. His fiancée can play with that bag of crazy.

We stand in silence for a few seconds, at which point I should've just left, but stupid here didn't. Changing the subject, I begin to inquire about the upcoming nuptials, and in true fashion, Diego salsa dances around the questions before he actually settles on an answer to any of them.

When I casually mention seeing her driving his car, the gaslighting begins again as he puts forth a valiant effort to convince me that it wasn't his car.

I remember it like it was yesterday. I had a giant bag of Skinny Pop popcorn, even though my dietitian *hates* when I eat it straight from the bag, totally ignoring the portion control we're working on. As I was getting my porch prepped, I noticed Diego's car pull up at the stop sign. I hadn't seen him in months, not even driving past. His windows are heavily tinted so, unsure if he even noticed me, I did the standard head nod of acknowledgement. No honk, nothing. As the car slowly continued through the intersection, I noticed that the back window was down and there were kids in the back seat. At that point, I could tell there was a woman driving that car. He would never in a million years let some *random* drive his new car. That's just further proof that he had been involved with this woman for a good minute while he was still playing dirty games with me, even though he continues to deny it.

Then, right there in the produce section, I let Diego know that seeing his car drive past made me think of the last time *he* drove past. So just to fuck with him, I ask if he remembers. He smiles, looks away and adjusts his manhood. *He remembers because it was something naughty he'd never done before – with me, anyway.*

It was just after our infamous s'mores encounter right before he vanished. I was fully engrossed in another good book, so it took me a little while to notice that Diego's car was pulling up to the curb. Anyone else find it hilarious that he was accusing other men of showing up so frequently at my house when *he's* the one constantly showing his unexpected little face?

He approached with way too much swag, distressed dark denim shorts and a snugly fit charcoal Adidas tee with a matching ball cap and sneaks. No person wearing just normal clothes should look that good.

He made it to the top of my porch but didn't approach me. He just stood staring at me for a few seconds while a cocky little smirk formed across his face. Strolling toward me with his water in hand, he gently removed my blanket-covered legs from the Ottoman and took a seat on it, facing me.

I did speak to him. I said hi, but he never replied. He simply took a seat, still with that naughty grin plastered on his face. He boldly slid the blanket down from my waist to peek underneath. At that point, I could only assume he was smirking because he knew I didn't have clothes on under that blanket. After a shower, I have been known to throw on one of the many mens' button-down shirts I own with a matching pair of Victoria's Secret panties and my ankle socks, because these pampered soles are never bare. Usually when I'm in the house, that's my standard attire, but I occasionally sneak outside in said attire because damn it, it's *my* house. If I want to sit on my porch with no pants on, that's my prerogative. I am usually covered with a blanket, relaxing, reading a book. *My* house. *My* life. *My* business.

Despite noticing that I was outside with no bottoms on, he still hadn't said anything. He just kept smirking while he traced one finger teasingly up my inner thigh, inching ever closer to my honey pot.

I inhaled deeply, then removed his hand because it was only 7:30 p.m. The sun was nowhere close to setting and my street was very much still bustling with traffic, pedestrians walking their dogs... Hell, my neighbor was literally across the street unloading an entire minivan full of groceries with her husband. So the absolute last thing this man was going to do on this porch today was have a special conversation with my lady lips.

"Not a chance, buddy. Don't even think about it. Look!" I pointed down the street to my left. "Three people *right now* are walking down the street with their dogs."

Diego glanced over at them, then back to me, examining my face and pretty much everything else with his intense, soulful eyes. He smirked again, which made me *so* nervous, then simply got up and walked into my house. Like what the actual fuck? I couldn't get up yet because the neighbors were passing by with their four pups, waving and chatting with me as they always do, and I didn't have any pants on.

Just as they were about to walk away so I could get up and investigate what the hell was happening in my home, Diego stepped out onto the porch and smiled at the ladies. Of course, they all swooned.

He retook his place on the ottoman facing me and pulled out my favorite black bullet.

"Oh, so you went in there to play in my toy box?"

Still not a word spoken. He clicked it once and attempted to hand it to me.

"Oh, absolutely not." While my orgasms with my battery operated boyfriend are not nearly as intense as when Diego provides them, they're still no joke. They still get pretty loud, and the fact that he would be sitting there with all of his sizzling sex appeal watching me, it would only turn me on more, which isn't helpful.

Still facing me on the ottoman, he pulled the blanket off my lower body, tossed it behind him and swiftly lifted my legs to drape them over his knees. My legs open and feet no longer touching the ground because he's so much larger than I am, he clicked the toy again and tried to hand it to me.

"I wanna watch," he finally said enticingly as he licked his full lips, then slowly leaned in and planted a very soft kiss onto mine. A low "mmmm" rumbled from his broad chest when he "accidentally" grazed my lady peach with the pulsating toy, which caused me to audibly exhale and instinctively grab onto his forearms. I pulled my pelvis as far back as I could from the rhythmic sensation assaulting her and continued my verbal objections because, like, how many groceries does one family need that they were *still* unloading that damn van?

He clicked the toy once more, "Quiero ver," he repeated, this time en Español while stroking his two fingers up and down my smooth outer thigh. The heat emanating from his smoldering eyes ever so clearly indicated that he was not leaving until this happened.

He then unknowingly pressed the bullet to the exact part of her that would absolutely finish me, which caused me to exhale sharply and contract my entire midsection like I had been gut punched. Now that he knew he'd found the spot, that's about to be a wrap. I hate it when my body betrays me and reveals all of my secrets. This hateful man continued through all the settings on this toy, slowly teasing me until he reached number fifteen, which he knows is my preferred pulsation. He held the toy up again in front of me and repeated the phrase that he'd been saying this entire time. But this time it was, "I'm *going* to watch."

By that time, I was deliriously horny and my lady juices were soaking all the way through those lace panties. At least he didn't rip them off this time. He grinned wickedly and placed the device in my hand, compelling me to hold the thrumming vibrations inescapably against my spot, and watched in fascination as it only took a few additional seconds for me to lose my entire shit. I almost had a stroke trying not to scream out. Hell, I probably looked and sounded like I *was* having one with all the twitching and grunting I was doing trying to hold it all in while the neighbor waves at me from across the street. He had enough forethought to restrain my other arm so we wouldn't have another fire table incident like the last porch visit. I dropped the toy to the ground, still buzzing, as I was wheezing heavily trying to catch my breath. He picked it up, turned it off, and set it on the table beside me. "In case you need it again."

This man then lifted my ass ever so slightly off of the chair and slid the black lace panties off of my quivering body. After deeply inhaling the essence of them, Diego smirked, put them in his pocket, picked up his bottle of water, and left without a word. Who the fuck does that? I promise he needs to be the one asking about my therapist, not all these twisted bitches I'm friends with.

He revels in the memory with a goofy smirk on his face and a slight protrusion of his gray sweats that he tries to cover with the groceries he's holding. When the time comes to part ways in the store after the emotional rollercoaster of the mini argument, the reminiscence of naughty memories, and the mutually shared tension, Diego opens his arms for a hug. I lean in for that church lady embrace, which is so formal and weird because I'm used to having my body fully pressed up against his, but today I don't. And this is the first time that he has never grazed, fondled, or playfully squeezed my breasts after a hug, so maybe there is hope for him yet. We both turn for that last lingering glance as each other walks away.

CHAPTER 15
only my spirits should be ghosting

I wake up to my phone vibrating so much that I thought maybe I left my toy on overnight. I reach over to see what's going on and it's my Facebook notifications blowing up, because apparently my dear dysfunctional friend Brie saw a man's photo in the comment section of a popular celebrity's post. It was asking what single men are looking for in a woman, and this very handsome man replied with answers that she rather enjoyed. She thought it would be wise to tag me in the post and tell this man all about me. She did a pretty good job with the description, if I do say so myself.

But for real though, *you have got to be freaking kidding me right now.*

As I'm picking up my phone to call her to find out what the hell she was thinking, my phone begins to ring and, of course, it's her. Since she traveled over to the west coast, it's six a.m. there, so she's on the phone with me, sounding like she's full of testosterone since she just woke up. In a gruff voice, she tells me about this man and how he's just in the neighboring state and is so handsome and has beautiful teeth just like I do... and seems to be able to punctuate. Apparently, she has stalked his page and is now sending me screenshots.

I can't disagree. He is a fine specimen of man – milk chocolate, chiseled, with beautiful lips and a perfect smile. And don't even get me started on that salt and pepper facial hair that makes me lose my mind.

"What were you thinking?" I grumble

"You're always telling me to find you a man! I just found you a beautiful one! Message him!"

"Are you crazy? I'm not messaging this man from a random post."

"What the fuck is your actual problem? That man is fine as hell! Message him!"

"I know, and he's gonna have every woman in America in his inbox."

"So what? *Message* him!"

"Ok so they're all going to be prettier and hotter than I am."

"Are you for real talking yourself out of this before you're even *in* it?" Brie asks in disbelief. "MESSAGE HIM!" she snarls.

"Yes!" And *OMG did this bitch just growl at me*?

"Ok, but what if they *are* prettier? So what? Are they more educated than you? Probably not. Do they have their shit together? How's their credit? Do they have seven baby daddies? Are they even single? Are they just gold diggers? Do they even use proper grammar?"

"Wait, since when is that a criterion for dating?"

"It is for *you*! Don't act like a man who knows the difference between 'your and you're' doesn't get you hot!"

"Ok, big facts." I give in. "Fine. I'll message him, but I am absolutely telling him how weird you are and that this was *not* my idea."

I uphold my end of the bargain, and now we wait. It's in The Universe's hands now, which worries me some because lately I feel like this bitch has the dropsies where I'm concerned.

I'm trying to figure out what the hell is *wrong* with these men!!?? Or better yet, what's wrong with *me*? I've still been kicking it with Hassan, totally against my better judgement. If you recall, he's the one who ate all my red starbursts while *watching* me shovel in the frigid cold without lending a hand. He's also the one who came to my home to visit with food only for *himself*. Still trying to figure *that* one out. But we've been hanging out as friends ever since because he legit lacks the courtesy to be able to date me.

I cook out? "Sure, you can come git'chu some food."

You need a ride after dropping off a moving truck? "Sure, I'll pick you up."

Cable goes out for two days during the Olympics? "Sure, you can watch track and field finals here – two days in a row." That's what friends do, right?

So imagine my surprise when I asked if I could sign into his Netflix account right quick to watch something the other day, and this fool told me, "No. those kinds of passwords are only given to family. Sorry."

Wowww, are you for real right now!? It's freakin' *Netflix*!! What the whole hell am I going to do in there other than watch *flix* on the damn *net*? He acted like I asked for his social security number. Now imagine my total and utter confusion when this *same* fool wants to borrow my all seven of my box-set seasons of True Blood. *Well*! Guess what!? "Seasons of True Blood are only given out to family members, sorry."

See? The dropsies.

All of this *after* I had taken him out to see Gary Owen at the Improv. He was funny as *hell* – lots of new material. Laughed 'til we peed, so it was a great show even though the service was *horrendous*! Afterward, on the way to his car, we were accosted by a questionable-looking man in a du-rag and an old leather coat – never mind that it was easily 80°.

He had an expired license incoherently babbling about *his ID, $12, a jitney,* (but I think he needed $23 for that so he couldn't get the ride), *white people always look at him like he's crazy* (newsflash, so did we and we ain't white), *and professed that he could just TAKE their money but that wouldn't be nice.* We couldn't tell if he was asking for cash or a ride, though I suspect he wanted both. I was listening to this hot mess thinking to myself, *oh man, I hope this fool don't try to rob us! Lived my whole life in the projects, never been robbed. One night in Pittsburgh...* Meanwhile, *this* nut I'm with had his feet in an open fighting stance, just staring straight ahead, watching this stranger out of his peripheral vision while leaving *me* to do all the talking. Can you say something please and handle this situation!?

That only further illustrated why I would never be able to seriously date this person. Men are so quick to ask an independent woman if she's even capable of handing over the reins to a man in a relationship. I have no problem with that, as soon as I can find a capable one who puts me in a relationship where I don't have to *be* the man in it! I want to be the *girl* for a change – I still have all the parts for it!

Saying *I'm beginning to lose hope* is the understatement of the year! I haven't had a solid mutual connection with anyone in years – since Amir. He and I spoke all day every day, pretty much sun up to sundown outside of our actual jobs. We would meet in the weirdest places, like McDonald's at 6:30 a.m. before his 12-hour shift just so we would get to spend some time with each other. So I double dog dare anyone else to say another word about me being "high-maintenance" because clearly, if I like you enough, we're at Mickey Dee's at dawn.

Amir worked a very physical blue-collar job, so of course I was a bit nervous inviting him to the company Christmas party, as I had never seen him actually dressed up before. After seeing what some of these men deem acceptable date attire, can you blame me? When those double doors swung open and that man showed up, bald head, all 6'1" of him crisp from head to toe, I almost lost my footing. Candid photos of us were taken, some of which we were in the background and we looked like we had known each other forever. You would have never thought we had just met less than two months prior. I was feeling this man so much that he could get it. *All of it.* And I am *never* ready to give anyone the panties that soon after meeting them, but he could have gotten the entire Victoria's Secret collection. I just needed some up-to-date paperwork, please.

We celebrated Valentine's weekend together since the actual holiday fell on a weekday. I made dinner and a picnic-style dessert on a blanket in front of the fireplace. I even gifted him an entire hour of Blaire's magical hands – and we all know I don't share my massage time with just anyone. He also bought beautiful roses and thoughtful gifts. The most meaningful words were written in the card that he gave to me, which almost never happens. On the actual holiday, he came to my job to tell me that he had to go to work out of state. Two people had died on the site, so they were short-handed. He brought Dunkin' Donut holes for Dani and me, had lunch with me out in the town square, passionately kissed me goodbye, and I literally never heard from Amir again.

The outright bewilderment among my mother, my friends, and colleagues who all just saw us a week earlier at the company party was at an all-time high. No one could understand why this seemingly polite and well-designed man would just ghost a woman. Yes, I called, texted, even hand wrote a letter because how, when everything seemed to be going so smoothly, did we go from "I could see myself sharing a life with this man" to him disappearing? The only thing anyone could possibly think of is the fact that I asked for STD results and happily provided mine, however he got his done but never reciprocated. He *said* everything was ok, but I wasn't going to take his word for that. I showed him all of mine; I wanted to *see* his.

As part of my Valentine's gift, I knew for sure there was going to be an envelope full of paperwork in that gift bag so we could check that fireplace lovin' off my bucket list. But alas, there was not. So the consensus among the group was that something was wrong in that paperwork and he just didn't want to share, so he would rather disappear than be honest about what was going on below his belt.

I was so distraught, depressed, and very nearly destroyed after that because how am I supposed to open up and permit myself to have actual feelings for someone again, trusting that they're not going to just vanish? And with every single person I'd met after that, it was so much harder for me to let my guard down and not wonder when he too, was going to disappear.

It took three years to meet another man with whom I felt a connection like that. Frederick showed up with red roses on a first date, which had never happened before. Though my preference is yellow roses, I was just tickled that someone was thoughtful enough to bring flowers at all. We talked in person for hours! I found him to be incredibly handsome and was very much attracted to him despite some of the other things that I would consider disqualifiers in anyone else. I was convinced that if the show *Married at First Sight* came to Pittsburgh and we both signed up, I felt very strongly that they would have matched us. And then, out of nowhere, for no actual known reason, he vanished as well. Frederick was also someone who would not have had to wait very long for sex because of the connection that I felt between us. The way he looked at me, his endearing smile, his touch, our intense conversations, the laughter we shared, just an explosive chemistry that I didn't often feel.

After reconnecting with him down the road, I learned that he wasn't over the situation that resulted in him being a newly single man at the time. I get that, but ghosting is never the answer. He could have simply said that he wasn't ready and I would have understood and, honestly, I might have even waited for him because connections like that don't occur every day.

But how can I be expected to form a connection when I get messages from men like:

DaWoogie69: Confession: I am a cheating fuckboy and my punishment was to go on Omegle all night and let people laugh and take pics of me while I wear a bib and pacifier.

I mean, I'm all about some confessions but *damn*, I literally don't even know what that means. I'm intrigued enough to post it to my Facebook page so someone can explain it. Why can't I just get a *normal* online message? Then there's...

MarkieMark08: Hello hello good morning I'm Marq wyd p.s. don't cheat on me

If this is how you need to start a message to someone, do I *want* to explore anything with you?

My follow-up questions would be; why does everyone you meet cheat on you? And what makes you think I would? I am many things and have a few good flaws, but the one thing I'm not is a cheater. Ok, well, kinda once, but it totally doesn't count. OMG that sounds like something a cheater would say, but hear me out.

My ex and I hadn't seen one another for almost a month because of his work/daddy duties. So, as a surprise, I showed up at his workplace, fully intending for him to have his filthy way with me in his spacious car. Yeah, it was daylight, but I was young, dumb, and down for whatever back then.

Jeremy's unkempt brows rose when he noticed how the breeze made my long straight hair flow when I strolled through the automatic French doors of the café. I was absolutely hard to miss in my black pea coat and leather stilettos.

He immediately left his post in his kitchen and rushed to my side, licking his enormous lips in anticipation. With his gangly body and big ass bobble head, Jeremy definitely wasn't a looker, but the way he carried himself, combined with his deep baritone voice, really drew me to him. Instantly, Jeremy noticed that I was wearing no visible bottoms. As he slid his hand up my thigh, his eyes widened when he realized he didn't *see* bottoms because there *were* none – just my Victoria's Secret lace-top thigh highs.

In that instant, I noticed his tall sous chef's hat was soon not going to be the only stiff thing on his body. With his hand still on my thigh, he asked, "Did you for real come to my job with no clothes on?"

I leaned into him while sliding his hand further up my thigh until it was on my bare ass, then whispered with a smirk, "Absolutely. And you're gonna fuck me in the parking lot."

Young and dumb.

I glanced over to the left where I noticed some poor soul with his woman, diligently trying to not stare at me because it was ever so clear that I didn't have on clothes and had zero shame.

"I'm working, though," he said nervously.

"Take a break."

"But it's daylight out."

"What's your point?"

"We have *cameras* out there."

"Then *drive* me somewhere *else*! I drove almost an hour with no clothes on," I whispered. "Are you for real making excuses right now?"

Baffles the mind because there were no excuses to be made when my mouth was wrapped around his hair-trigger dick while he was driving us to the movies one afternoon. Besides, Jeremy is the same man who I was telling Jenna and Marco about who consistently lasted mere minutes. So what the hell was he afraid of? He'd be done before anyone could even figure out that he'd even left. Again, young and dumb. Try that shit with me now, you will be politely dismissed.

We both noticed the eyes and reactions of the male portion of the couple adjacent to us. He seemed to be trying to figure out how this man could be in his right mind, making excuses to *not* have sex with the smokin' hottie who came to his job half naked. So Jeremy pulled me aside to the corner, away from the customers.

"It has been over three weeks since we've had sex. What is going on?"

"I'm sorry. Nothing, it's just I've been so busy with work and I've had my daughter."

"You do not have your daughter every day, so stop! And I show up at your job in this..." As I began to unbutton the three closures on the coat so that he could see the sheer black lace bra and matching crotchless panties, he stopped me.

With his manhood as hard as that calculus class I failed in undergrad, he informed me that they were tremendously busy in the kitchen and that he could not get away to meet me in the parking lot. Then he offered his apologies again while trying to adjust himself to make his raging erection look less conspicuous. While the man couldn't last long, he definitely had that long thick D. So typical – men with large power tools who don't know how to wield them.

"Fine. But I am clearly horny," I reprimanded while guiding his fingers onto my moistening essence. "So I'm putting you on notice right now. If you do not come over and get in these guts by 10:00 tonight, someone else *will* be by midnight."

He inhaled, tilting his big ass head and shot me a look that clearly said, *Liar. You love me way too much to have sex with anyone else.*

As the master of the one eyebrow raise, I exhaled and shot him a look that said, *bitch, try me.* Under normal circumstances, he'd be right – I definitely loved him, but I was tired and frustrated. He and I were not in an official, committed relationship. So, in reality, either of us was free to do whatever we wanted, but I am a loyal person. If I'm sleeping with you, you're the only person with whom I'm sleeping. In many cases, if I'm even just seriously dating you, you're the only one. I have never had the time nor energy to spread myself that thin with multiple men. But in this situation, I was just exhausted from whatever this game was that he was playing. He wasn't committed to me, but didn't want me to have anyone else. He didn't appreciate me and clearly took me for granted way too often. Maybe he and Diego are related.

I've never been a person who was after a man for his money because I would prefer his time, attention, and affection. But Jeremy wasn't even giving me *that*, so this was where we were at. I could have left and had sex with anyone in that store the way I looked that day, so he was either gonna come and handle this action, or find out how many men there were in line who couldn't wait to pick up the ball he dropped.

Of course he called but didn't come, so I absolutely called his bluff and had sex with my former classmate Jace, who had been making eyes at and flirting with me since we met. We had many classes together, but despite Jace's advances, I had remained faithful to Jeremy, who clearly didn't value it. So Jace slid through, literally, and delivered lovin' that lasted way longer than Jeremy's ever did. That's when I realized, *oh, sex can actually last longer than like six minutes*? He was only the third person I had ever had sex with, but it didn't seem to matter how snug or slippery my snack box was; he was able to hang, so what the hell was Jeremy's excuse?

Needless to say, Jeremy was super pissed when he found out, but that's not my issue. He really had no right to be. I literally put him on notice, making it perfectly clear what was going to happen, and he elected not to believe me. Thus, I don't consider that cheating even though I did technically have sex with someone else. That shit was totally preventable. He was even more bent out of shape when we had to have that delicate discussion regarding his lack of stamina when it comes to pleasing a woman.

Add to my TO-DO list: Petition to have Merriam-Webster's definition of cheating changed to allow for special circumstances

CHAPTER 16
i'm going straight to hell

Desirée and I don't get to see each other nearly as often as I would like. Since she homeschools her children and doesn't drive, we're at the mercy of the school schedule and her husband's work schedule. But that doesn't stop us from talking on the phone frequently and acting simple as hell. All the shenanigans from our college days together continued right on through adulthood. Except, we use better judgment now. Because clearly, as you just read, back in college, I was the posterchild for the equation young + dumb = bad decision making.

We find ourselves reminiscing about that psychotic time when my college boyfriend Brent and I broke up. After a year of dating, it was pretty heartbreaking and devastating. I didn't realize what a good thing really was because I was so new to the dating world. Knowing then what I know now, if I could have a re-do, I would change so many things. But not about the girl who thought it would be a good idea to move into my dorm room and then pursue my *very* recent ex. Desirée used to say, "that girl know she wrong as two left shoes!" Michele knew damn well we were together – the entire campus knew because it was very small. He was someone who every woman wanted, yet I couldn't figure out why *he* wanted *me*. I was still a virgin who was nowhere near interested in parting with my special gift just yet. Meanwhile, there was a line of women just waiting to throw it at him, and I wouldn't be surprised if he caught some of it. Literally freshman year, one locked herself in *his* dorm room and threatened to harm herself. Like seriously? These are the lengths you're willing to go to when you *know* he has a girlfriend? And do you think these actions make you more or less desirable in the mind of a teenage boy?

Were there people built better than him? Absolutely. He wasn't some large, chiseled structure. Were there people better looking and smarter than him? Not many. There was something about him and the way he giggled. It was just really appealing. His beautifully shaped, rounded lips didn't hurt either. I imagine those were a few of the reasons my new roommate was so interested in this man.

Desirée took a strong stance that if Michele was interested in him, then she should *not* have moved into my room. A sentiment with which *every single one* of my friends there agreed. I asked her multiple times to find a new room and move out if she was going to pursue him. I was congenial in my request because my mother raised me to use my words *first*. And while I may be a *kind* person, I am not really that *nice*. So the shit got ugly when she decided she was not going to leave and was going to date Brent anyway.

Because the campus was so small, there was no shortage of people who knew about the situation. Most of them were on my side because that really was a fucked up thing to do. At one point, the mortuary sciences chick, who I wasn't even that close with, was leaving messages on our voicemail of a song and every time I would come back from class, I would be all pissed off when it started playing, "He's mine. You may have had him once, but I got him all the time." It was Desirée who informed me that the message was not intended for me, but for Michele. She said that I needed to listen to the entire song, He's Mine by MoKenStef, which spelled out how you might be with him now, but I'm a whole better bitch than you are and I will *always* be on his mind.

When this chick had the audacity to ask me if I had a black sweater she could borrow so she could go out with *my* ex-boyfriend, that's when I was like okay, this bitch done lost her whole damn mind. So I started taking the cordless phone, the remote, and the cable cord with me everywhere I went. Super petty. But it was my television and my phone so, go buy your own. I would also deadbolt the door at night when I went to bed if she wasn't there. I left her out there knocking a few nights. Every time Michele did laundry, she would come in, dump it out all on her bed and leave, and I would take two of her socks – obviously not a matching pair. So eventually she just had a bunch of mismatched socks and couldn't figure out why. I would also leave the bathtub faucet pulled up so whenever she turned on the water it would come out of the shower, which for Black women's hair, that's not ok and super petty, but I didn't care. She shouldn't have been in my room – that's all.

It started to get real when friends would come to visit and we would all be hanging out on my side of the space. She would walk in and a hush would come over the room. They would just stare at her, so eventually she would leave. One of them made the observation that I kept all the pictures up of Brent and me. We had amazingly adorable pictures together from the college events and outings we attended, and there is still not a couple alive who photographs as well as we did together. I had no intention of taking them down. I wanted her to look at the stunning couple every day because she would *never* look as good with him as I did.

There was a darkness in my friends back then. Michele once brought a bagel with a sour cream and chives type topping back to the room. When she sat it on the desk and walked away, my friend went over and put it upside down on the floor and then back on her plate. We only vacuumed maybe twice a month, if that, because our floor's vacuum was usually broken. So whatever was on that floor was unnoticeably attached to and blended in with the topping on that bagel. When she came out of the bathroom, picked up the plate, took a huge bite of the bagel and walked out of the room, everybody about died.

But it got extra dark when I was informed by one of these friends that she had used Michele's toothbrush to clean the black ring around the inside of our dorm room toilet. Not sure why, but the toilets on our inner city campus consistently had a ring, regardless of how often you cleaned them. I promptly went out and brought a new toothbrush that I kept hidden, just in case someone considered doing the same to mine. Though Michele didn't seem as unstable as my friends or myself, you never know.

So the day that Des and about three other friends were in my dorm room, Michele walked in and brushed her teeth. When I tell you the entire room almost vomited on each other? I couldn't figure out why they were all acting so dramatically until someone looped me in on the madness. I mean, I thought they were just using my bathroom like any normal person would do. How could I anticipate that any of them would take it upon themselves to "clean" the toilet for me? The twisted chick who did it just sat giggling with pride and the rest of us were like, we need to keep an eye on your ass because you're not wrapped all the way tight. I *did* in good conscience buy a new toothbrush and left it on Michele's desk, but I don't know if it ever got used.

I absolutely drew the line when another friend wanted to put Nair hair removal cream in a giant vat of my roommate's perm. Not because I had sympathy for her or didn't want to damage her hair; Michele was an attractive girl with beautiful dark chocolate skin, so she would probably still look good without the hair. It was purely selfish. I was the roommate with access and a crystal clear motive. I watched enough crime TV to know that I'd be the first suspect if they found hair removal cream in her hair products.

Once the semester ended, Michele promptly relocated. That was definitely in her best interest because my friends were *not* going to stop coming for her and I was *not* going to stop them. If Desirée had just put a curse on her back then, none of that would have ever been an issue.

We laugh, reminiscing about those good ol' days when we were being so bad. But now, since she's found the Lord, *I'm* now the bad influence in the friendship. I'm fine with that.

Add to my TO-DO list: Have Desirée say some prayers for a li'l extra forgiveness for me because Karma is probably not my friend right now

CHAPTER 17
i am not the bank

It feels like I am being awakened by ringing phones more often than not lately. I'm definitely gonna have to turn on silent mode. The phone announces the caller as my mother, so I reluctantly answer. When it's this early in the morning, she will almost certainly have something weird to say.

I answer, still in that partially awakened daze, "Morning, Mother..."

"Morning sweets!" She's super excited. "One of your gifts is arriving today!"

"Is it a husband?"

"Nooo..." she says with genuine sadness. "It's not even a penis in a box."

"Ok, see. I gotta go now."

She is cracking up like this is a totally normal mother/daughter conversation. Well, I guess it is for us.

"Well wait, did your spirit lady come?"

"My what?"

"You know, the spirit lady you said that was supposed to come last night."

She's talking about Katriona, the Reiki Master I met on Instagram. I had ordered some gemstone bracelets and when we discussed what parts of myself I was trying to heal with those particular stones, she suggested I try Reiki.

I don't know much about it other than she uses her hands to deliver and improve the flow and balance of energy to promote healing. After reminiscing with Des about those college days, I could use it! A few of my friends have it done regularly and really seemed to enjoy the experience. I read somewhere on the internet about it helping with fertility so I figured, why not? I have spent so much money and put in so much effort, at this point, I have nothing else to lose by trying something alternative.

"She didn't knock you out and steal the TV did she?" my mother asks in the most serious tone ever.

I must know, "What is *wrong* with you?" I have no clue why she is always so worried about someone stealing my televisions. They're all wall mounted, so it'd take a while. "No! It was *fine*. It was actually quite relaxing, and that was the longest my brain was not active, like ever. So it was very rejuvenating."

This petite, adorably exotic, raven-haired beauty came to my house with a box full of crystals that she felt would help with that particular region of my body. When I first saw her, I couldn't help but think to myself, *why does she even use filters on IG? She's prettier in person and really doesn't need them.* I escorted her to my basement, which was candle lit and illuminated with red Himalayan salt lamps. Though I was super curious about everything she was doing, I didn't really say *too* much. I just kind of had a lot of thoughts happening. But once she started saging the basement, I had to ask to make sure she wasn't re-summoning the Spirits of the Damned. They've been pretty quiet for a while now. She confirmed that the saging would in fact eliminate said spirits. *Well bitch, where were you nine chapters ago when Carol Ann and the damn poltergeists wouldn't come out of my television set? You're the white girl I needed here!*

She informed me that during the process, when thoughts come into my head, she wanted me to acknowledge them and then move them out. And I thought to myself, *shit, if this is an hour long, all I'm gonna be doing is moving thoughts out of my head because I literally can't stop thinking about everything. Especially since I'm nosey and I always want to know what's happening.* I fully anticipated being hyper-aware of everything that would be happening, but I agreed to the process. If this chick could move some energy around and open up whatever chakra is in, near, around and/or blocking my baby making area, I was all in. *Let's do it!*

The relaxing music played while she began working on my wayward energy. OMG the thoughts would literally not stop, but I had to move 'em out.

How did she get her liquid eyeliner to go on that flawlessly? When I use liquid liner, I look like a total wackadoodle – it gets everywhere. Ok, stop thinking about that. Let it go.

Dude, her eyebrows are so perfect. Mine are actually perfect as well, but hers look fuller. I wonder if they're real? She's kinda exotic and a lot of exotic-looking people are hairy. So those could be her real brows. Why is this on your mind right now? Stop it. Move it out.

Did she just place something between my boobs? Not that it matters. There's probably popcorn and cookie crumbs in there anyway. I could deliver snack time to an entire daycare class with the amount of nibblets that get lodged between them. OMG. Stop it. Move it out.

Is she touching my feet? I should have warned her I have a slight foot fetish. Stop it. Clear it out.

Oh boy, I think she's putting crystals on my belly, which has been pretty round lately and full of angry air. If one rolls off my mountainous midsection and breaks, do I have to pay for that? Stop it. Let it go.

What if I actually do let it go and pass a little gas if I get too relaxed? That might be embarrassing. Nope, definitely embarrassing. Ok, stop. Let. It. Go! No wait, DON'T let it go, hold that one in.

Oh boy, she's doing some pressing and tapping? Is she summoning the dark forces to my womb? Of course not. What's wrong with you, Renée? Stop it, let it go.

And just as quickly as all those thoughts came, they all disappeared, and the rest of the session I spent in a completely mindless relaxed state with not a single thought running through my head. It was absolutely the freest and clearest I have ever felt.

Afterward, she told me that nothing was actually wrong with my sacral chakra, which is the one that is affiliated with my reproductive region. I wasn't sure if I should be pleased with that news or disappointed considering that every physician I've seen so far had *also* told me that nothing was wrong in that area, yet here we are. I guess I was hoping physically everything was fine but energy-wise maybe she could fix some broken link and then I might have success? But as it turns out, my entire lady region is a ray of fucking sunshine. Great to know.

My heart chakra, on the other hand, apparently has the Great Wall of China surrounding it in an effort to guard myself against the hurt from previous love, probably the pregnancy losses I've suffered through, and I'm sure some of my daddy issues. So everything she said made total sense. My poor therapist...

"Well, I'm glad it went well and that you finally got some relaxation that you needed," Mama says. "What's going on today?"

"Kash asked me to go kayaking with him this morning, then I made a chiropractic appointment for after, because my back is always a wreck post yakin'. And for some weird reason, my hips have been bothering me."

"You sound older than me right now."

♀ ♂ ♀ ♂

As I watch Kash approach me at the docks of the North Shore, I come to the stark realization that he and I can never have sex. Unfortunately, he reminds me of my paternal unit, who we recently found out was adopted. After a little Ancestry DNA research, I've learned that *his* father, my bio gramps, was *also* a rolling stone spreading his seed all over town with no regard for where it landed. He *also* didn't take care of his children with any regularity. So clearly that apple didn't fall far from the proverbial tree. Hell, it might still be attached. There is no amount of money that can convince me that this handsome man isn't my cousin somewhere down the line.

As we rent our two solo kayaks on the date that *he* requested, it gets real extra quiet when the woman gives us the balance due of forty dollars. I glance over to see if he's getting ready to pay this woman, and he begins to pat his body, looking for his wallet.

"Oh, uh... you mind grabbing this? I seem to not have my wallet."

Of course you don't. Why would you have a name like Kash and not have any? *I could always tip his kayak over once we're on the water.*

The entire time we're getting fitted for our life preservers and getting the quick water lesson, his phone is ringing off the hook. It continues until we are pushed out into the water on our kayaks, and he finally answers it. The call is brief, and then another, and a third.

Once we make it out a few meters, I begin to feel like the ghetto version of that old Cinemark Statement. Y'all remember the one from about eight years ago that we all had memorized because it came on before *every* movie for about two straight years? Or maybe I just saw too many movies.

Our world is overrun with technology; there is a time and place for it. But kayaking down the Allegheny River is not the time NOR place. "OMG" and "*LMAO*" *with your baby mama on a bright little screen while floating down a river disrupts those AROUND you. You know who you are and SO DO WE! We want our renters to ENJOY their kayak rides, FREE from distractions. Do NOT be the person I have to smack in the damn head with an oar, BECAUSE I WILL! No talking or texting during a water excursion. If you have a baby mama emergency, please step the hell away from me and take the call, otherwise IT CAN WAIT!*

Ok, yeah I *definitely* watch too many movies.

Kash argues with this chick about custody, child support, and her "trash ass boyfriend" the entire way down the river until we make it to the fountain at Point State Park, where his phone finally falls into the flowing water. Thank you, Water Goddess, for sparing me that drama all the way back up the river.

I take some pics and ask if he cares if I post them to social media. He confirms he's good and that it's ok to tag him.

Once we return to the docks, he has the nerve to ask me, "So, you wanna grab a bite?"

"Sure! Next time when you bring your wallet, we can eat wherever you'd like." I give him a quick hug and head to my car. I'm tired. My name is not Bank of Renée Savings & Trust. I'm tired of supporting the endless line of broke ass dudes who inevitably find me. I can afford to date my man. At this stage in my life, I need someone who can do the same. If you ask me out, you should be prepared to foot the bill, just as I am when I take *my* man out. Come on!

♀ ♂ ♀ ♂

I pull up to Dr. Jake's office so he can put my spine back together and see if he can do anything about this chronic hip pain. He has me lying on my back with his hands on the interior of my bent knees. This is the most excitement any part of my inner leg has gotten in a while.

"Squeeze your knees together," he requests with his strong Louisiana drawl.

"Oh shit, something popped!"

"Where?" he asks, confused, because he didn't hear it. "In your hip?"

If I could blush, I probably would. "No... In the... Middle... Central... Area?"

Now his pale skin begins blushing too as he tries to maintain his composure and deliver a reasonable explanation. "Ok, well, in the center of your... pelvis, there's actually a joint there that can become misaligned in people with hip issues."

"So... What you're saying is... You just adjusted my va-jim-jam?"

He looks very pensive and nods slowly. "Yeeeah, pretty much."

We both just look at each other in silence, then burst out laughing! It was the type of uncontrollable laughter that draws people to want to know what's happening. Blaire, who works in his office as his primary massage therapist, comes running into the room to see what crazy thing I've done now to send us howling. I explain that Dr. Jake just broke my snack box.

"*Fixed* it! I *fixed* her snack box!" he shouts, then pauses, realizing what he just said and shakes his head in defeat. This is why he has to adjust me in a private room away from the other patients.

"Well, that's a relief. I thought you accidentally called 9-1-1 again," Blaire says, which just sets off another round of hilarity.

I have so much tension in my upper back and neck that when he works on me, he usually has to do some deep tissue massage before he can adjust me. It felt really good but it also really hurt because of the inflammation. I was holding my cell phone and apparently there's a certain combination of buttons that if you squeeze them on the side of the phone, it automatically sends an emergency message out to your three most dialed contacts. It sends them your geographic location, fifteen seconds of a recording, and some sort of emergency message. So in the middle of my adjustment, I couldn't figure out why my phone just started blowing up! All of a sudden Brie, Liza, and my mother are all calling and texting because the recording they heard was:

Uuuuungh, that hurts! You're hurting me...

OK but it's tight. I have to get in there... just relax.

But it's gonna hurt... Nooo, you can't...

And then the message abruptly cut off. I legit had no idea that this safety measure was a thing. And what are the odds that my fingers would have pressed the two buttons that send this emergency cry for help? I don't even know what the combination is to be able to recreate it. I'm just thankful they all called *me* first instead of sending police to this location, because I can only imagine them busting into this establishment for what they presumed to be some sort of hostage situation, only to find me being adjusted. So now I no longer hold my phone when the good doctor works.

"Did you tell Jake about our last massage?" Blaire asks.

"Hell naw!! I'm still traumatized and my throat still hurts!"

Dr. Jake gives us a look of, *do I even want to know?*

Blaire begins to enlighten him with *A Tale of Two Ta-Ta's*. "I always go to the bathroom to wash my hands while she removes her clothes to hop under the covers for the massage."

"I had everything off," I interject. "And was ready to slide between the heated sheets when Blaire starts *screaming* bloody murder! So I covered what I could of the world's largest breasts with my forearm and hand and run over to see if something is trying to kill her."

Dr. Jake is looking back and forth between us as we both tell this story in dramatic fashion.

"She flipped on the light and came rushing in and I'm all like, 'dude, you're naked!'"

"No shit! Why are you screaming?"

She stabs a finger at my vanity two feet away. "There is a *massive* spider in your sink! Like, I thought it was the cat!"

I slowly tried to peek my head in, but I didn't see the spider. Then when I finally *did*, I started screaming and then *she* started back up again too. The thing was *huge*! I don't even know how this giant wolf spider got into my house because I don't recall him knocking on the door and me letting him in, because that's how big this damn thing was.

So I ran over and with my free hand, grabbed the bottle of Clorox Clean-Up that I keep near the other basement sink and shove it at Blaire. "Spray it!"

"Your house, your spider bitch! What the hell are you handing it to *me* for!?" she shrieked.

"You have a better vantage point! And clothes on! Kill it!"

"I can't! It's too big! And stop jumping! You're gonna put an eye out with those things!"

I repeatedly yelled for her to turn on the hot water as I was spraying the shit out of this poor defenseless spider and I honestly felt *terrible*. He probably was just like, 'Hi, my name's Ed. Just here to eat some bugs. How are you guys? Love the decorative towels.' Meanwhile, we're screaming and flipping out, spraying him in the face with bleach. I felt *so* horrible. I usually will catch insects and remove them from the house, but what do you do with a spider the size of your palm? We already know the lengths I went through for the chipmunk.

Dr. Jake is cracking up at our hysterics.

"He was so large that, at first, he wouldn't go down the drain, but when he finally did, Blaire stopped the water and we stood, totally out of breath, staring at each other and at the drain full of bubbles. I was still panting with my arm and my hand covering the massive bosom of life, praying there's no nip slip."

Blaire loudly and dramatically interrupts with full arm gestures, "Then, out of noooowhere, a thick hairy leg comes out of the drain and up through the bubbles! Mother fucker came back to life like Michael Myers!"

"We both started wailing, jumping and spraying *again*, turned the water on full blast, then pulled the drain closed."

Still breathing heavily, Blaire looked to me and said, "You know that damn thing probably had a wife and like ninety babies, right?"

What a bitch!

As we exit the treatment area, Blaire hands me my purse and phone, which alerts me to a new message.

"Are you gonna check it?" she asks, then turns to Dr. Jake. "She gets the *best* online messages!"

"Umm, I don't know about 'the best'," I laugh. "The last few have been fairly normal, though."

Siiiigh, never mind. Forget I even said that.

Some lovely soul has decided to send me a poem he's written. This becomes the point when I feel like I need that emergency button combo – *send help!* I hand her the phone and Blaire reads the sonnet aloud.

When lonely feels like a hell
And I couldn't get one to ring the bell.

Simply staring at pretty face like you
Wouldn't get a remedy for my love flu.
I decided to jot down these few lines
Thinking you would feel the heat of my illness.

"OMG this man *clearly* doesn't know that you're a raging germophobe who would sooner chew through your own arm to get away from his hot contagion," Blaire jokes then continues reading.

Every time I come across your picture
I started shaking, filled with shiverness.

"Wait, what the hell is a 'shiverness' and he just stopped rhyming?" she inquires, puzzled, looking to me like I'm the one who can make sense of this fresh dose of crazy. She continues on.

If you are not picky down to preferred genes
I am here for you as one potential choice.
Seeing is believing 99 percent of the time
Let you decide the make the day dating with me.
- Advil

Yes, this fool's name is Advil. I CAN'T! These two are doubled over in laughter, and even the patient in the waiting room who overheard the whole thing is giggling.

"This never gets old," Blaire says, handing me my phone.

"It does for me!"

♀ ♂ ♀ ♂

After an exhausting day on the water, I'm just ready to finish my day off by the fire as soon as it's cool enough to light it. And I don't wanna hear shit from nobody – just let me be! My mail lady, Shayna, strolls up onto my porch. I am at the end of her route, so she and I often get to chit chat because she's no longer in a rush at that point. She has a devious grin on her face, like she's about to start that aforementioned shit that I said I didn't want.

"So remember that video you posted a while back on Facebook about the chipmunk that was in the doctor's office?"

"How could I forget *that* deranged shit?"

She hands me a stack of mail. And then just leans back on the ledge to view my reaction. Of course, front and center is what very visibly looks to be a bill from that doctor's office.

"You have got to freaking be kidding me right now!" I immediately rip the envelope open to see if it's what we think it is. She's been delivering mail for well over a decade, so she knows what the hell a bill looks like. And since all I ever get in the mail *are* bills, I know one when I see one as well.

Sure enough, these people had the nerve to request a twenty-dollar copay for that visit where I helped save them from the mating calls and rituals, followed by the reproduction of chipmunks in the office. I know it's a fertility office, but we've got to draw the line somewhere.

"Hold on!" I go in the house, grab a sharpie, and write "DO NOT OPEN! CHIPMUNK INSIDE!" across the bill, place it back in the envelope, tape it up, and write "return to sender" across the front of that bitch. I hand it back to her to take with her because I have no intention of paying it. Of course, I will call them tomorrow morning to iron that out, but I just really needed to be dramatic about it first.

After spending a peaceful evening immersed in my new L.C. Son vampire novel, I have completely lost all track of time. I consider staying out just a tad longer until a strange woman approaches my home and confirms that it's time to take my ass back in the house.

"Excuse me. Do you have another cigarette?"

"No, sorry, this is a cigar."

"Ok, thank you."

She walks away but then returns from another direction about ten minutes later.

"Excuse me again. Could you do me a favor and help me out with something?"

Probably not at 11 p.m. "Like what?"

"Do you have extra money for me to get groceries?"

WTF? Am I being Punk'd? Why is that a question I'm being forced to continually ask myself? *Hell naw,* I don't have grocery money for this random woman. A bitch here got *four times* my mortgage in student loan debt. I'm trying to make sure I have grocery money for *me*!! Plus, if you're out here walking past my house trying to bum cigs in the middle of the night, I'm thinking you're not using that money for actual groceries.

Between co-pays, bills, broke ass men and randoms, I'm going to erect signage outside of my house that reads, "I am not the bank!"

Add to my TO-DO list: Get a good attorney on retainer so I can punch the next person who asks me for money

CHAPTER 18
are you talkin' to me?

"Holding my phone – dead air on the other end. I was just hung up on because this dude is for real salty with me because I've known him a mere two months and don't consider him my '*friend*.' There are people I've known *years* longer than him that I don't consider 'friends.' Associates? Acquaintances? Sure. But for my handful of *friends*, I will hit Lowe's for the shovel, a circular saw, bleach and/or lye, lay a tarp down in the trunk, help hide the body, then alibi the shit outta their ass all while joining the search party to help find the "missing" person. So I ask you, sir, where are we on that spectrum of coffee acquaintances to murder alibis? You ain't there yet. Though I will say one of my friends and I already have an alibi set up just in case – can't say who though because that would totally defeat the purpose.

Before I can even set the phone down, it's ringing. Ohhhh, do I have a bone to pick with Miss Diana here!

I answer not with a hello, but with, "Are you trying to ruin my life?"

"What are you talking about?"

"You suck at this swiping almost as much as I do!"

"Seriously!? I thought I did well. Damn," she whines.

"Yeah... not so much! The one last night told me that my profile was cute and funny. That being said, he would have to come back to me when he got his teeth fixed."

"Ok," Diana says. "But at least he's self-aware."

"Bitch, you just *wanna* get hung up on, don't you? And the other one, well, he didn't treat his dog well, so he's automatically out."

Okay, maybe I am being a bit too picky here. But I feel I am well within my rights to be completely turned off by and not want to date the man who leaves his dog outside all day in this type of disrespectful heat and humidity. I got an attitude in the fourteen seconds it took to get my mail and it's just on the porch. So *you*, sir, need kicked in the throat, and if I had your address, I would absolutely call animal control on you. Talkin' 'bout some, "he has water and is in the shade." Really, asshole!? He's also covered in hair. You are talking to a woman who risks her electric bill to leave the AC on for the cat *inside* of the house.

"Ohhhh noooo," Diana agrees. "Totally unacceptable. But someone has to be at least a little normal."

"Yup. So normal that he sent me this. Hold please." I send her a screen shot of the message I got a few hours ago that reads:

Hello very beautiful lady. I ride by your home on purpose just to see your Beautiful face. However I'm not dark skin so I'm not comfortable stopping just to say hi. I realized your working from home just like me but at the same time I don't want to appear creepy not me. Your very attractive tho, I would like to get to know you? If at all possible. Just so you know it took me 2 months to let you know this. Have a blessed day.

She reads in silence, then I hear a long exhale, "So this man has been driving past your house daily for the past two months."

"It appears so. And he recognized me from this profile."

"Well, at least you look like your pics. But when exactly did you specifically request a dark-skinned man?"

"That would be never. I enjoy all flavors of chocolate. And a li'l French vanilla."

"Well, that's pretty creepy. Maybe you should stay off your porch for a while. I was just calling to see if you could design the logo for my new PR company."

"Sure. I'll send over the contract – as soon as I amend it to say that you're no longer allowed access to my online dating apps."

"That's fair." She laughs as we end the call.

If all of that's not bad enough, now Facebook is notifying me of an inbox message from a woman rudely questioning me about why her fiancé is in photographs with me. *Umm, isn't that a better question for your fiancé?* If he is in fact engaged to you, *he* knew that. *I* didn't. That's right, Kash, the man who told me it would be perfectly ok for me to post our water photos and tag him in them. Makes sense now why he was mysteriously untagged in all of them just a few days later.

Based on her messages to me, I don't believe this woman is his fiancée. Could they have been dating and possibly even more? Absolutely. She's an attractive woman. Naturally, I stalk her page for any indication that these two were even remotely serious. There are zero photos of them together, but mysteriously, there's a vague engagement announcement posted *after* our kayaking pictures. Very convenient. She continues to provoke me by arguing that they are, in fact, engaged and she's in his bed right now – that I should call his phone and *they* will answer. It's too early in the morning for this bullshit and I didn't sign up for any of it. I just want one normal person to love and kayak with, and now I'm in the middle of this dysfunctional triangle. But I'm feeling particularly ballsy this morning, so I call her bluff, pick up the phone and dial his number.

It's ringing... Still ringing... And as I suspected, no answer. So I try again, just for kicksies. Nothing.

Before replying to her message so she can take her messy ass up out of my inbox, I text Kash to confront him about this alleged entanglement. The entire time while she is messaging me back in an effort to prove their commitment to one another, Kash is steadily texting me that he is not engaged to that girl and that she is nothing but a fan who wants him. Pardon me for interjecting this observation, but Kash has, in fact, sent me an unsolicited dick pic, so she must be fangirling over something else. I'm done with this and blocking both of them.

♀ ♂ ♀ ♂

My mini bestie, Julia, is in town and I can't seem to get her out of my vibrating bed. She just lays there across the foot of it moaning. Swear if she climaxes in that bed before I do, there's gonna be some problems! I'm also confused as to how people are able to get *so* comfy in my home. So comfy, in fact, that everyone's bowels seem to need to move as soon as they arrive *here*. What they all neglect to realize is that my main bathroom doesn't have ventilation, so if it's a ripe one, that odor *will* follow you down the stairs and swiftly permeate the living room. And if you *think* you're safe going in the basement where there *is* ventilation, well I regret to inform you that the previous owner didn't have the good sense to ventilate it *out* of the house – just *up* into the ceiling so it sneaks into the dining room. Secret's out.

Jules is getting extra comfy in an effort to make up for lost time. She hasn't been up north for over two years because of the pandemic, but since covid rates have declined, she decided to bring the family up to Pennsylvania for a visit.

"So how's your helpful hunk?" she asks in the most innocent, yet devious, little tone.

"My what?"

"Your hottie therapist…"

"Ugh, not you too! I thought I would have at least *one* friend who wasn't obsessed with this man."

"Sorry, you were gravely mistaken. Have you discussed your aging issues?"

"Bitch, I know not of what you speak. Okay!? My birthday cake still says I'm thirty."

"Bitch, your birthday cake is *lying*."

That was probably the funniest thing I'd heard all week because Jules *never* swears! I fill her in on how therapy is going, how my overall desire to fight my boss has been curtailed and, of course, this man's chiseled shoulders.

"Does he have any insight into these dating issues of yours?" she asks.

"I mean, he laughs a lot. I don't think he's *supposed* to, but you almost can't help it and I don't even blame him. I'm thinking that, though I *have* my own set of issues, I'm not the *actual* issue here. Look at *this* insanity." I open my phone. "I'm being totally normal here."

Julia takes the phone from me while she's still vibrating in my bed.

Tank007: I thought you were off today.

Me: I have a freelance marketing & design business with a laundry list of work to get done before Friday.

Tank007: My mouth, these lips haven't done any "laundry" in months.

Tank007: They like to wash panties. Sorry. If you block me I understand.

"I'm not sure if you should be flattered or freaked out," she says with a look of utter terror on her face.

We stare at each other in silence. "Definitely freaked out," we both say, laughing in unison.

"Did you block him?"

"No, but I definitely deleted him."

Though Diana's swiping abilities have left much to be desired, there have been a few who have been able to engage in solid conversation. One left his number, so I called this morning. I don't normally do that, but what the hell, why not?

Ok literally... What the *hell*!? Why is it *so* hard to find grown ass men who don't live with their *mothers*? While leaving a message on the voicemail I thought was his, an older woman picked up to talk to me! Really!? I'm over here thinking I'm calling his cell phone, but nope, it's his mama's landline. On her old-school answering machine, she heard the voice of a "lovely young lady," as she described me, and felt compelled to pick up. She politely informed me that it's time for her son to settle down and get the hell outta her house. Oh, and that his cell phone was cut off. She just threw his business all out in the streets.

Lady, I am so sorry, but I'm not the one for your son because if he's *still* living with *you* at 46 years old, you need to just keep him. What these men (and some of their mamas) don't seem to understand is that budgeting for a house, paying bills, up-keeping said house, it's all a lot of *work*! When a man jumps from one girlfriend's house back to home, to the next woman's house, then back home again, he's never fully learning these skills because there is always someone essentially taking care of and picking up after him. I'm neither your mama nor the maid. So if a man has never lived alone, he will not be living with me.

"Right!? So if he can't keep his own phone on, I'm seriously doubting he's living at home to help his mother with *her* financial situation," Jules says with a laugh. Then the shit gets real. With sheer and absolute panic in her voice, "OMG the bed stopped! *The bed stopped!*"

"Well, it has a thirty minute cut off," I remind her as I hit the button once more. The vibration begins to soothe her and all is right with the world again. Well, in her world maybe. Mine is still a total shit show.

I tell her about the dude who I was flirtatiously asking to bring me some Swedish Fish. You know, the candy? This man went bat shit crazy! He went all the way off about how me always asking him for stuff tends to be a sign that I would only want him for what he can give me. Fool, I asked for some Swedish Fish, not the damn Hope Diamond!

"I hope you told him that with your current credit score, you could buy the entire candy store," she jokes.

"Real talk, I *knew* he was never gonna *bring* me Swedish Fish anyway cuz he has no car! So in that instance, why not just play along like, 'yeah baby, I got you'?"

"Especially since *every* time you guys go out, you'd have to pick him *up,* so the *least* he can do is grab you some .99 cent candy. I don't feel like that's asking much."

"You're right. But any guesses as to what's *not* about to be happening right now with these gas prices high as giraffe kidneys?"

"You constantly picking him up?"

"Good girl. And don't even get me started on the guy who walked through the threshold of my house, looked around, and said, 'you don't even need a man; you seem to have everything together.'"

"What!?" She sits up in shock, then lays back down once it begins to wear off.

Is my four-bedroom home spacious, clean, and well decorated? Absolutely. But is it some mansion in the heights of Sewickley? Not even a little. It should by no means be intimidation- or emasculation-worthy. I have no idea how that translates to me not needing a man. Despite my accolades, I am the first to acknowledge the need for a man. I just don't need him to pay the mortgage. However, look. If he wants to throw something down on this gas bill that is Satan's best work and higher than my SUV payment in the winter, I'm not going to argue with him. But there's a host of other things for which a woman needs a man that aren't financially related. So I'm not sure where this idea came from that a man's value is solely financial. I have my own money. Would yours help? Of course. But what I really desire is a man's time, attention, affection, sense of humor, loyalty, support, understanding, presence, and, of course, the ability to make me come until my straightened hair curls back up on its own. Sadly though, it's beginning to seem like it's easier for a man to just offer his money than that laundry list of *free* attributes.

Jules hangs out and vibes while I fill her in on my upcoming date tonight, and she catches me up on her toddler daughter who decided she *needed* to know how the babies get into a mommy's tummy. Despite their parental efforts to duck and dodge the question, it could not be put to rest until she received what she deemed a viable answer. I promise this child is smarter than most adults I meet.

♀ ♂ ♀ ♂

For my date tonight, I am rocking dark denim skinny jeans, a sexy off-the-shoulder sweater, black heels, and my standard Tiffany's accessories. My hair is laid, face is beat, and my waist is snatched – I'm ready for business!

Jeff shows up in sweats... to the restaurant. Oh, and lest we forget the matching cloth ball cap also made of sweat suit material? I can't make this shit up. I didn't even know they *made* sweat suit ball caps.

I try to hold my tongue but it comes out like super judgmental word vomit, "Oh, we're casual tonight?"

He nods like it's the best possible attire in which to make a first impression at a restaurant – where no one else can be found wearing sweats. I try to look past it, but Jeff here looks like a giant yellow crayon! The yellow sweat suit *under* the yellow sweat jacket and the yellow cloth ball cap is just fuckin' me all kindsa *up*! I find myself wondering if he has matching yellow sweat suit socks and undies beneath this look inspired by House of Big Bird.

Since I'm not a big drinker, the bill only comes to $55. Jeff eagerly takes the $22 that is left on my gift card, which more than covers what I ordered. He covers the remainder with his card, then *this* chump throws down four dollars for a tip like he's doin' something!

"You are *not* leaving this girl $4 on a $55 bill." Especially when *he* didn't even have to cover the *whole* bill himself! I have no idea why I consistently end up out with men who are either too cheap or just don't understand the concept of tipping at least twenty percent.

He ponies up $5 more – again like he's doin' something. I discreetly drop five additional dollars onto the pile as we depart because we received excellent service.

He asks me to accompany him to the mall that's just down the hill. I agree, since I would like to pick up a few things. Swapping my heels out for my comfy Chucks, we swing by the store to get a case for his phone. It's $18. He then attempts to talk this man down to $9. Boy, this is RadioShack! It is not up for negotiation. *If you don't just pay this man and quit being cheap!* I have no interest in being associated with this level of instability, so I go wait out in the hall.

Wait, it gets better. *Then* I bought a Yankee Candle that I'm carrying in addition to my giant purse. We go to the kitchen store where I purchase one small item. Jeff takes *that* bag from the cashier to carry in a weak effort to appear gentlemanly? So I laugh. "You wanna carry a bag for me? Did you really just take the tiniest, lightest one!?"

This fool looks at me, smiles, and says, "Yup. But you should be fine to carry that. You have pretty manly physical characteristics anyway."

Wow... Definitely not sure how to respond to that one. *This man is clearly blind. Just play it off, Renée.* "Ok well, maybe my shoulders. Cuz I have traps that all the boys envy," I reply playfully.

He looks me up and down and says, "Eh... not just your traps," then continues walking down the hall.

Really? FYI, I would *never* date a *man* built as curvalicious and fly as I am! If all this sexy is how a *man* is built, then just start calling me Raymond.

But I guess that's not as bad as when the one guy told me he looked through my Facebook photos and found some of me a few years ago.

"You looked amazing! Your body looked so *different*! I mean, you were sexy *as hell*! You're sexy *now*, but then, wow! I woulda married you *and* drank your bathwater! *What happened*!?"

What happened? Really!? Wow.

"How long ago were these photos taken?" I asked.

"Umm, about twenty years ago."

"Oh ok, back when I was still a *child*! Of course my body looked different and better then!" We can't *all* stay as lean as *his* genetic predispositions.

Even though I owed this person no explanation, I calmly informed him that fertility medications are not friendly to the female body, so I am now the proud owner of a few extra pounds.

Add to my TO-DO list: Book a flight to the west coast to beat Diana's ass

♀ ♂ ♀ ♂

On my drive back home, my ringing phone jolts me out of fantasies of strangling Diana and back to reality. Before I can even say hello, it's my mother. Talking... about anything and everything. It literally doesn't stop. So I just focus on my ride home and listen to her yammer on about her car, her colleague's cat, the dead possum she found in her closet ceiling. She really needs to report her landlord. She finally asks, "How was the date?"

"He was dressed like a banana. Next subject, please."

"Well damn. Ok then, how'd the rugs turn out?"

"Great actually. When the carpet cleaners finally moved the couch, I found six toys under there!"

"*Sex* toys!? Well what the hell are they doing in the living room!!?? Don't you have a special place for those?"

"OMG *six* toys, Regina! That the cat had batted under there and we thought were lost for all eternity."

"Oh! Well, you know my hearing is going. And you *are* kinda freaky, so one never knows with you."

"Really Mother? Anywayyy." I sigh dramatically. "The guy came the other day and started the porch carpeting as well. It looks soo nice so far!"

"Wow, so now you'll have to break the porch in... again..." she says, cracking up.

"Yeah ok, it's time to go. Love you, bye."

I hang up while she's still cackling in my ear. She's so filthy. If anyone cares to guess where I got it from – right there. She's not wrong, though.

Add to my TO-DO list: Take this next exit to Lowe's. Porch shades! NOW!

♀ ♂ ♀ ♂

With my new tan shades in tow, I finish my ride home from Lowe's in silence, wondering why in the hell it's so difficult to find "my person." I worry that I'm seriously going to die alone and try as I might, there is nothing more I can do about it. Giving up sounds like a viable option right now. Deciding that I'm throwing in the dating towel and setting fire to it, I turn on my radio, volume on high, open my panoramic sunroof to let the cool air in, and belt out my 90's R&B jams. I couldn't carry a tune if I had a bucket, but if you think that's about to stop me, think again!

Not sure why my car thinks I need to *hear* to back up, but the volume automatically drastically decreases as I reverse into my driveway. That doesn't prevent me from continuing to sing like I'm being paid for this concert. While I gather my items and the headlights fade out, I notice a gentleman approaching me in the darkness.

What a sight for sore eyes. "Gemini! Ummm, hi..." I giggle bashfully. "Sorry you had to hear that," referring to my singing voice.

"Hi there." He smiles shyly. "You sound better than me, so it's cool. I don't mean to bother you –"

"No, it's ok. But why are you back here?" Y'all know my paranoid ass is over here thinking he came back to rob me and steal those TV's my mom is always worried about.

"Oh damn, this is all one house? It's so big I thought that maybe this was your entrance to your apartment within the house. You used this door when you came out to help me, so..."

I can't help but laugh because the way these homes are set up here, that's completely possible. If only he knew my past living situation, he would know that I will *never* live attached to anyone else ever again.

"No, this is all me. I don't see your bike."

"Yeah, it's supposed to rain this evening, so I drove down on my way to my cousin's house."

"Oh, well, if you'd like to pull around front and meet me on the porch?" I offer.

I run through the house like a crazy person trying to straighten up in case he has to use the bathroom or something. Male company was *not* expected.

I make it out to the porch just as he's pulling up to park a completely blacked out Tahoe. All I can think is damn, how is it that every man I meet who is not necessarily trying to date me has the flyest car on the planet, but the ones who *are* trying to date me just don't even *have* one? Instead, they have license issues or DUI issues or budgetary issues or the completely strange ones who literally just don't have a license. How do you live with no license?

He strolls up onto the porch and hands me a card. "It's nothing much. I just wanted to show my appreciation for your help a while back."

"That is so sweet, thank you!" I gush while opening the thank-you card. In typical male fashion, it's not signed or anything, but there's a gift card in it for Applebee's. What an incredibly sweet gesture, considering I received a message from a man this morning who told me that I could pick any two items off the Taco Bell dollar menu that I wanted. Sir, no thank you. If I'm going to Taco bell, I'm leaving with at least $13.72 in food. *Your* cheap ass can stick to the dollar menu.

Gemini stayed and engaged me in great conversation for about two hours this time. He left with my business card that was sitting on the fire table. I still don't know this man's first name, but hopefully he uses the number because I would really like a ride. On the bike, of course... I mean, and maybe...

Add to my TO-DO list: Figure out Gemini's real name, then see how handy he is because these porch shades may need put to good use sooner than later

CHAPTER 19 - BONUS

two wrongs don't make a right, but...

Who steals plants out of someone's yard? I had five stunning flowers arranged in an arch at the corner of my property and one is just mysteriously missing. I immediately open my Ring doorbell app to see if it caught anything. As I hastily scroll through all the motion events on the app, my scrutinizing narrowed eyes begin to bulge in shock. "Ohhhh myyyyy shiiiit," I slowly moan.

I instantly pick up the phone to call my sister, Neka. It just rings and rings then goes to voicemail, so I redial four more times until she finally picks up.

"Uhhhhh," she groans. "Is Nan okay?" she asks, her voice still thick with sleep.

"Yeah she's fine but you-"

"Then why the fuck are you calling me this early in the morning!?" she interrupts in a loud deep yawn.

I can always count on her to be belligerent in the early a.m. hours. She's even worse than Ariah.

"Girl somebody stole flowers outta my yard-"

"Hol' up, I *know* you ain't call and wake me up outta a good ass sleep to talk about no damn flowers!"

"Bitch would you just wake up and *listen*?" I snap back. "Okay so someone stole flowers outta my yard, and I went to look at the motion events on my Ring to see if I could make out who did it. Whyyyy is there an entire half hour of me and Diego very *clearly* gettin' nasty on that camera!? My legs are all up in the air convulsing like I'm wavin' to someone across the street with my foot!" I exclaim. "I'm officially a porn star," I whimper, hanging my head in shame.

"Da fuck!? On the porch!? *Again*!? Wait! So what happent, he called off his engagement!?"

I pause before continuing, "Not exactly. He was supposed to get married a few months ago, and it never happened. But they're still engaged."

"Well damn, I'm awake now!"

Deafening silence falls between the two of us.

"Well bitch, talk!" She demands. "Was it an accident? Did he trip and fall and his mouth landed between your legs? Talk! Cuz I thought you said you wasn't gonna do it!"

Sigh... "No accidents. It was quite intentional. And yes, as much as I lecture you about some of your dirty deeds, I was not right in this situation at all. I did it."

"Well that's for damn sure. But to me, he was *way* more wrong. You don't *know* that girl. *You* ain't put a ring on her finger and commit to her. *You* did not have intentions to love, honor, cherish and be loyal to her ass. *He* did! *You* ain't the one sneakin' around out here lyin' to cover your tracks every day. *You*, ma'am, are single. If you wanna spread your legs for every man in that zip code, *you* are not committed to annnyyyone and that is your prerogative, though I wouldn't advise it."

"I mean that's true, but I shouldn't have let any of it happen in the first place."

"Well he shouldn'ta been sniffin' around *requestin'* that any of it happen. I *know* he had to be the one to kick off these sexcapades because you ain't gon call *him* to ask for it wit'cho punk ass. I'm about to look 'em up on social, gimme some names."

I give her the info, then I wait quietly because I know she's about to have some shit to say.

"Damn," she hisses in disbelief. "Ain't Diego like *your* age?"

"A few years older. And can we *not* say it like I'm ancient, please?"

"What!? So he's about to marry a *child*? How *old* is this girl?"

"Like *half* of his."

"Fuck out of here! You have *got* to be kidding me!? So he ghosted you two years ago and made this girl a child bride? Does he need to be called 'daddy' that badly!? Like, does it for real need to be *literal*?!"

"Exactly cuz he's definitely old enough to be a father to her *and* all them babies she got. And it's crazy because the stuff he and I laugh and joke about from our childhoods, she couldn't even begin to comprehend because she wasn't even *born* yet!"

Silence falls once again as I presume she's reading additional posts.

"Wow. Wowwwww... So he's just out here making this little girl look real stupid while she's postin' he's her Earth, her wind, her fire and everything in between, meanwhile he's out here making a seven-course meal out of your snack box!? Sorry, but you know you probably ain't the only one right?"

"Oh, I'm aware." I admit. "He would *always* tell me I'm the only one yet, somehow I seemed to *never* be the only one. So there are probably a bunch of side chicks all over town and we're *all* mysteriously the 'only one,' I'm sure."

"So sis... I don't get it. You're like one of the smartest bitches I know. Why the *fuck* do you keep allowing this narcissist back into your life? I'm so confused."

"Girl, me too," I reply in emotional defeat.

Narcissist is accurate. Google should probably delete their current definition and replace it with a full-page, 3-D, color photo of Diego's ass. But the harsh reality is I have feelings for this man, I always have. And those feelings, unfortunately, are not conducive to me making solid decisions, even when I *know* the likely outcome. So any pain he has caused me is just as much my fault as his, because I keep *letting* him walk back into my life and inflict it.

A few months earlier, I was on my porch working when that familiar Dodge pulled up to the stop sign. I hadn't seen Diego since we parted ways in the grocery store.

"Heyyy ma," he shouted from his car with his alluring accent. "I got a business proposal for you."

Immediately I was suspicious, but mildly curious. "Are you gonna get outta your car and talk to me like a normal human?"

With a nod of his head, he pulled off leaving me to wonder what the hell just happened. Moments later, he strolled up onto my porch and pulled all of the shades down. Not wanting to be noticed on my very heavily traveled street, he sat facing me with his back to the shades after parking his easily distinguishable car around the corner.

"So what is this alleged business proposal? A new venture? You need some design work done?"

"Nooo, but you can make a few hundred extra dollars a week... I don' wanna ask though cuz you'll probably say no."

Well that made me even more suspicious, because what could he possibly have me doing that would allow me to make that much extra money without designing anything? "Ok so, *noo* I won't have sex with you. *Noo* I will not grow weed in my basement for you. *Noo* I will not be some lady pimp for a gang of ho's you might be runnin'-"

"Wait... what ho's? *What*-"

"*Noo* I will not have your baby," I continued without missing a beat. "*Noo* I will not get ordained and marry you and your infant girlfriend. *Noo* I-"

Diego jumped in, "Yo, where you gettin' all 'at? It ain't nunna those things."

"So then what is it?" I inquired skeptically.

There goes that pesky silence again - it filled the porch as he contemplated how to tactfully word this "business proposal" of his.

"I--- would like to-- *pay* you-- to resume..." He then licked his smooth lips and averted his eyes down to my lady region.

Who the hell could've seen *that* coming? "Wait, *huh*? Come again?"

"Yes, exactly," he immediately interjected with a sly grin forming on his lips. "I would like to make you *come again*... Over... an' over... an' over again."

Eyes wide, mouth open, completely blown away, not even sure how to respond, I was so incredibly confused. "So you want to *pay* me to dine south of the border? Why!?"

"What'chu mean, 'why?' You know I love her," he smoldered, inching closer toward my partially open legs. I crossed them in response.

"You have an entire fiancée at home who you can do that to for *free*. Why are you here offering to pay *me* to do it? And that's like a lot of money... And you just want to-"

"Yes," he interrupted. "And you're right, but it's not tha same wit' her."

"What does that even *mean*? Like I seriously need clarification because it makes no sense to me. Does she not finish when you do it? Does her lady space taste like garbage truck juice? Like what is the issue?"

"I don' know; I can't explain it... it's jus' not tha same. *She's* special. I always told you that. No one cums like you do."

And he *has* always told me that – so have many other men. But that doesn't mean I understand it.

"I miss you," Diego continued. "I thought about you ever since we ran into one another in the store, an' I miss her as well."

Brows furrowed, my mouth hung open in disbelief because in my mind, this man had been planning to stay faithful to this girl. Clearly I was delusional.

"Okay I gotta run, but think about it, and I'll stop by next week to see what you decide."

Diego stood and walked toward the steps. We maintained some sort of twisted eye contact - his sexy, mine bewildered, as he strolled off the porch, down the sidewalk, and around the corner until he was out of sight.

Beyond baffled by all of this, I did what *any* normal woman would do in that situation. I called my mother! Okay so maybe most normal people wouldn't do that, because most people don't have the type of relationship that Regina and I do.

"Hello my sweets," she sang happily as though she hadn't spoken to me in weeks, when in reality we'd just spoken two hours ago.

"Mom, I have a question. What makes a man want to *pay* to put *his* mouth on a woman?"

More silence. If I got paid for the amount of silence that has been occurring throughout this entire situation, I could retire in the south of France.

"Well are you ready to have this conversation?" she asked in this deep sultry tone like we're about to engage in some illicit verbal exchange for which I will be charged $3.99/minute.

"What the hell does that actually mean?" *I feel like I've been asking that question far too often lately, as well.*

She continued, "I'd once found myself in a similar situation."

"Wait what!? You were paying men to suck dick?!"

"No, fool! I had a... *friend*. And that is literally all he desired. He would refer to it as the *Nectar of the Gods*." Her voice rang with so much pride and solemnity, I fully expected her to launch into a mystical African legend of how it all began.

"Hi, please hold while I vomit on the CAT! Are you freakin' kidding me right now!? I'm gonna be sick!!"

"What do you mean? We share."

"Okay but we don't need to share *this* much."

She continued against *my* will, "He would say that he woke up tasting the nectar and-"

"Okay no. Seriously, I'm really gonna be sick, like we can stop now. You are over *seventy*!"

"So I hesitate to say this," she persisted as though I had not requested an end to that sordid conversation.

"Yes, please hesitate... long, like as in *stop*!!"

"But you got it from your mama. That golden box is hereditary, my dear."

"Yep, and I am nowww hanging up. Love you, goodbye."

♀ ♂ ♀ ♂

The next week, Diego popped up as promised – probably the first promise he'd ever kept in his life! But when munching of the box is involved, I would expect nothing less.

I thought long and hard about his "business proposal." This is absolutely wrong and I should say no simply because it's not *right*. And if he wants to be out here doing messy ho shit, he should just break up with his fiancée and remain single. My sister on the other hand was like the naughty angel on my shoulder screaming, "Do it! Take his money AND get your orgasm, then go get your nails done." That's the advice I would expect to receive from her.

On the other hand, my mini bestie, Julia, was lecturing me absolutely *not* to do it! "He's just going to drag you back in emotionally because you know you cannot separate your feelings when it comes to that man... that large, exotic, *beautiful* man... so I kinda can't blame you for being tempted, but don't do it!" she finished fervently.

And she was not wrong at all. Y'all know I have always made horrible decisions when it comes to Diego, so why stop now? I reluctantly agreed to his proposal but eliminated the per visit payments, which my sister thought was stupid as hell. Her stance was, if he's going to give you the money, take it. I stood on the other side, maintaining that since I don't actually *need* it, that amount of money isn't necessary when I'm the one benefiting from the visit anyway. So we'll discuss some other arrangement that doesn't involve hooker vibes, leaving money on the nightstand every time he exits, like I'm starring in the sequel to *Pretty Woman*.

I just had three stipulations: Much like Julia Roberts in that movie, 1. I would not be kissing him. 2. There was to be no hugging, holding, cuddling, none of that, because I didn't need anything else drawing me closer emotionally to him. And 3. Just be honest. I was aware of his situation, so there was literally no reason to lie to me. *None!* We've known each other too long and we're too old to just be out here lying for no damn reason. So just tell me the truth this time around. He agreed.

He then wanted to negotiate a set number of climaxes per visit – for *his* psychological and egotistical benefit, not mine. I was ok with one. He snorted and suggested I be reasonable and at least consider six. When I could recover my voice, I politely declined and countered with two because we all know I be done destroyed the entire house if I came that many times in one sitting with that man.

We ended up settling on *no more than* three orgasms per visit.

Diego first started dropping by once or twice a week at night after work, then began incorporating daylight visits just to hang out and talk. Our conversations have always been pretty epic. He was doing okay respecting my boundaries initially until the one night after he completed service, he just got super comfortable and posted up in my vibrating bed, pulled me close against him, wound his enormous anaconda arms around me and spooned with reckless abandon, gyrating his "log" against my bare buns for additional comfort.

As much as I revel in being the "little spoon," I questioned what exactly was happening here because he had a fiancée at home, could he not go get this tranquil snuggle time from her? None of this should have been happening, but this extra emotional shit *really* shouldn't have been breaking through the cracks of our agreement. He went on to share that quiet affection was something he was not able to receive from her, as there were so many people in his fiancée's house, kids in the bed, etc... So much so, he listed that as the primary reason they were not yet cohabitating. Newsflash sir, what do you expect to happen *if* you ever decide to marry this girl? But hey, that's *your* problem; *you* made your choice - not my circus, not my monkeys...

His visits remained steady at night, but increased during the day to hang out and talk because obviously when your betrothed is the age of your *own* children, the conversations must be rather limited. He and I tend to have deeper exchanges that someone significantly younger couldn't even participate in, because they literally wouldn't understand any of it. You can't talk to a person in their twenties about what we grown folks did at 8:00 p.m. every Thursday night when we were growing up. It's just not the same.

We carried on with the arrangement for a while, experimenting with all kinds of new things like that vibrating butt plug that my sister sent on my last birthday. Highly recommend, by the way. I need to write an Amazon review for that thing. We continued to push the boundaries of our experimentation until the point came where I was centimeters away from having sex with him. Talk about the mother of all poor decision-making? He was engaged this time, I was ovulating and horny out of my *mind*, and there were no condoms. His throbbing manhood was knocking at my palace door and had he elected to barge his way in, I would absolutely have obliged. The little man in my tunnel would have served some hot tea and warm crumpets, then fixed up the guest room for him. We both maddeningly maintained a high level of control and did not, but that brief moment of lustful temptation could have been an entire mess – him engaged, me possibly pregnant.

The next morning when I was lucid and no longer in my horny haze, I decided that I was done with all of the naughties. If he wanted to continue our dealings and go further, he needed to be single. Though I was sure he'd absolutely continue to do his messy ho shit, it would no longer be with me, as I'm the only one who would end up hurt in this situation. Whether he decided to ghost me again because he actually follows through and marries this girl, or he just decided to ghost me because he's being an asshole again, it would inevitably happen and I would be crushed - yet *again*. I had to verbally remind myself that I'm a good woman who deserves to be loved fiercely, publicly and be more than some cheater's side chick.

Saddened by the conversation that ended our dangerous liaisons, Diego still continued to call and visit. But this time, with him came the love bombing - flowers, edible arrangements, chocolate covered pretzels, my favorite vitamin water, and my preferred cigars. Where was this level of attention when he was actually single, if he was *ever* actually single? Soon calls increased to the point where we would spend hours on the phone talking at night if he wasn't already over here hanging out on the porch. We weren't doing anything sexual, he was just here for the conversation and company that he should have been seeking from his fiancée, but was choosing to acquire from me.

Body language and facial expressions in addition to his own words, made it seem like he was so unhappy and that, on some level, he *knew* this May/December romance was a mistake. Marriage only has a 50% chance of success when two presumably like-minded people are attempting to make the effort. Add a significant age gap into the mix, along with a man who has issues that he acknowledges but refuses to seek treatment for, and that would impede the success of *any* marriage. When you add on top of that, a young woman who clearly either lacks the life experience or simply doesn't know him well enough to even be able to pick up on any of the aforementioned... I'll just say, I would love to be a fly on the wall in that home.

Regardless of what he's telling me about his overall discontent, Diego would *still* park down the street like a fugitive on the run, leaving his phone and watch in the car so as to not have his movements tracked, in case she happened to be paying attention. He was deleting texts and calls, so he clearly still cared enough that he wanted to be there. Or maybe he simply didn't want to get caught to avoid conflict and wanted the end of their relationship to be *her* fault and not his? Not a clue.

He also shared that he felt like she wasn't being completely faithful her damn self. I can't speak to any of that, but what I do know all about from my years of dealing with him is the art of projection. If *he's* doing messy ho shit, ER'body must be doin' messy ho shit - much like he accused me of doing and *I* wasn't even in a relationship with him. But nevertheless, whether or not she was loyal, Diego's cheating was far worse. He was having an entire emotional affair with me, in addition to the physical aspects. A man can lay pipe all over town and have no emotions involved, but for him to hug, hold, massage, and sit and talk to someone, other than his girl, for hours on end, he absolutely cares. There *are* emotions involved. However, of all the feelings swirling around in his massive well-structured body, respect was clearly not one he was capable of, because even though I specifically asked him not to, Diego continued to lie to me without a conscience. Lied like I couldn't even tell when he was lying - and for no apparent reason, about the dumbest shit. It was like the more I would reinforce that he didn't need to lie to me, the more he felt compelled to do it anyway. Make it make sense! My bad, I forgot – nothing a narcissist does will ever make sense.

He would tell me that he loved me fairly often and my response to that was always, *always*, "You don't know what love is. If you loved *her*, you wouldn't be here with *me* and if you loved *me* you would never have left me and put a ring on *her* finger." It's like the words were coming out of my mouth, hitting my brick porch and landing in my mulch to be washed away by the rain. It didn't stop him from disrespecting her by continuing to say it and calling me, "my love" all the time. He once posed the question, "If I were to propose to you, would you trust me?" My response came with zero hesitation, "Fuck no. You proposed to *her*, yet here you stand in my kitchen, after licking me 'til my entire *soul* left my body, and you have the audacity to ask me about trust?" That's laughable.

Did I have love for Diego? Though I would never *ever* admit this to his face for fear of how he would somehow use that intimate information to further manipulate me, absolutely. Don't ask me why; I legit have no actual answer, other than the fact that clearly one can't control who they're drawn to, otherwise I would have walked right on past him 25+ years ago. Do I believe that Diego loved me in whatever way *he* thought was love? Yes, I honestly do. But unfortunately, that's a toxic kind of love I neither deserve nor desire.

"Soo, what'chu gon' do with that video?" Neka slyly inquires. I can hear the smirk in her voice.

"Ummm, I don't know. I did keep it though. Because when his messy ho shit inevitably hits the fan... his lying is pathological. He will absolutely deny it ever happened. Yes, it did. He will say that it's not him. Yes, it is. He will say that I seduced him into doing it. No, I didn't. I have all the proof – texts, IMs, screenshots, everything."

"Do you think she's stupid enough to believe him over all your digital receipts?"

"Not a clue, but I may send you a copy on a flash drive in case anything *mysteriously* happens to me."

Add to my TO-DO list: Woman up and cut Diego the fuck off! This whole thing is more past due than my mama's cable bill.

THE END

EPILOGUE

I feel like I should be saying something that gives you hope that a brighter future ensues, but y'all, I got nothin'! This shit is dark. But I can leave you with those updates that they run at the end of each Real Housewives season:

The sexy man Brie found online for me finally ended up replying to the message I sent. We chatted and talked on the phone for a little while and that was it. I am tired of being the person responsible for initiating everything and would like a willing participant in the pursuit for a change. So if he steps up, I will too.

Jeremy, the ex with the quick D, ended up marrying his baby mama, who had four kids prior to theirs. He was quick to lie about being married when he ran into a *gorgeous* friend of mine and started asking about me – that is until his *wife* walked up and introduced herself as such – intimidated, I'm sure.

As for Diego, well, we continued hanging out, platonically, however he *continued* to unnecessarily lie. When someone sent me screenshots confirming his lies, he then lied about *lying* instead of simply admitting it, humbling himself, apologizing, and telling me the actual truth. Also finding out that he had been calling me AND his fiancée "my love" this whole time made me wanna retch. At least differentiate your pet names for all your women. Gah! He *did* end up finally breaking off his engagement, but that's for a whole other book.

I also never heard back from Gemini, however overly emotional Kelvin *stays* driving past...

The basement bathroom drain is still closed in case my eight-legged houseguest feels compelled to send friends. And the Spirits of the Damned haven't been back since – well, not since they unloaded the dryer for me and all the clothes exploded out and into the basket. Blaire and I shot out of that basement *so* fast!

For now, it's still me, my nutty (but dope) mother, amazing friends, my career, the porch, and my moody cat... Standards will continue to stay where they are until someone amazing is smart enough to snatch me off the market and move me to a Carolina, dammit! Until then, I'm done looking and have deleted almost all of my dating apps. Mr. Right will just have to jump through my window while I'm binging Netflix shows because this savage search for a soulmate has me spent.

If you've enjoyed this read, reviews on Amazon are incredibly helpful to authors. Please and thank you!

ACKNOWLEDGMENTS

To my readers, thank you so much for your wild texts, crazy emails, IM's, fun social media posts, recommendations and reviews! I appreciate your support!

I would like to thank my mother, Rhetta, for her unyielding encouragement and insane commentary that gives so much life and dysfunctional warmth to this creation.

My irreplaceable friends Ellise, Kathryn, Cindy, Jennifer, Jocelyn, Crystal, and Tracy who were all on hand around the clock with thoughts, ideas, inspiration, beta reading, or simply readily available to listen to me vent about this entire process. Thank you.

My alpha reader, Kimberly, I appreciate your time, effort, kinky word-play, willingness to always help, and especially your friendship and massage hands. Thank You.

The entire Instagram author community who are all so incredibly supportive with words of wisdom and encouragement (along with answers to my *many* weird bookish questions), particularly L.C. Son and Tiffany Andrea.

ABOUT THE AUTHOR

For over a decade, J.R. Mason has been engaging in a savage search for a soulmate, but instead, men just keep offering up book material.

Mason received her bachelor of arts in journalism and mass communication from Cleveland State University and her master of arts in advertising/ graphic design/ public relations from Point Park University. A full-time marketing specialist position, along with running a freelance design company keeps her quite busy and leaves little free time for her guilty pleasures – movies and massages!

This Ambridge native also takes joy in playing her trumpet, screenplay writing, travel, outdoor fires on cool nights (obviously), anything with real sugar in it (sorry, Danielle), and reading erotica or psychological thrillers.

Contact:

jrenecreative.com/confessions

Follow me on IG: author_j.r.mason

BOOKS BY J.R. MASON

Rom-Com:
Confessions of a Sane Single Woman (2020)
Soulmate Setbacks: Confessions II (2022)

Crime Thriller:
Stolen Pieces (2023)